Pen and Conscience

Uncle Tom's Cabin
and Mid-Nineteenth Century
United States

Pen and Conscience

by
MOIRA DAVISON REYNOLDS

McFarland & Company, Inc., Publishers
Jefferson, North Carolina, and London

Frontispiece: Harriet Beecher Stowe. 1852 daguerreotype.
Courtesy Schlesinger Library, Radcliffe College.

Library of Congress Cataloging in Publication Data

Reynolds, Moira Davison.
  Uncle Tom's cabin and mid-nineteenth century United
States.

  Bibliography: p.
  Includes index.
  1. Stowe, Harriet Beecher, 1811–1896. Uncle Tom's
cabin. 2. Stowe, Harriet Beecher, 1811–1896 — Political
and social views. 3. Slavery and slaves in literature.
4. Abolitionists in literature. 5. Women in literature.
6. Social problems in literature. I. Title.
PS2954.U6R4   1985   813'.3   84-42735

ISBN 0-89950-131-1

Printed in the United States of America

McFarland   Box 611   Jefferson NC   28640

To my husband Orland
with thanks for encouragement

Contents

Illustrations

Preface
and
Acknowledgments

Social reform is brought about in various ways. *Uncle Tom's Cabin* exemplifies the use of skillfully and artistically constructed propaganda that contributed mightily to massive reform. This book has been in print for more than 100 years; both praised and condemned, it remains an important facet of American heritage and culture. The background of *Uncle Tom's* creation and reception is fascinating, and I hope that I have done it justice.

I am indebted to many persons for help with this project. Professor Richard O'Dell gave me valuable advice at the start. Professors Richard Sonderegger and Earl Hilton have made many helpful suggestions. I am most grateful to Professor Russel Nye for reading and commenting on the first five chapters. The resources of Northern Michigan University's fine Lydia M. Olson Library have been available to me. The staff members of the Peter White Public Library in Marquette have been most helpful in securing materials, especially by interlibrary loan, and to them I extend my profound thanks.

Moira Davison Reynolds
Marquette, Michigan

"Slavery is founded on the selfishness of man's nature — opposition to it in his love of justice."

— Abraham Lincoln, 1854

1
Written in the Book of Fate

My dear, you must be a literary woman. It is so written in the book of
fate.... Drop the E. out of your name. It only incumbers it and interferes
with the flow of euphony. Write yourself fully and always Harriet
Beecher Stowe...

— *From a letter by Calvin Stowe*

In the Hall of Fame for Great Americans, along with the busts of
Thomas Paine, Abraham Lincoln, George Washington Carver, and
others who have influenced the course of this nation, stands the bust
of Harriet Beecher Stowe. Cited as the author of the antislavery
novel *Uncle Tom's Cabin*, written before the Civil War, Mrs. Stowe
exemplified the power of the pen in reaching the conscience of the
North. This is the story of *Uncle Tom's Cabin* and the events that
contributed to its writing. We begin at mid-century of the 1800s.

A northeaster was lashing the town of Brunswick, Maine, when
Harriet arrived there on May 22, 1850. She was 39 and expecting her
seventh child in about six weeks. Her husband, the Reverend Calvin
Stowe, was finishing the school year at Lane Theological Institute in
Cincinnati and would arrive later. His new position would be
Collings Professor of Natural and Revealed Religion at Bowdoin
College in Brunswick.

Harriet's 18 years in Cincinnati were not uneventful. Like her
brothers and sisters, she had gone there because her famous father,
Dr. Lyman Beecher, had dreamed of creating a New England-type of
seminary in what was then considered the West. In Cincinnati she
had taught school and had had her first literary successes; it was there
she married, bore six children and buried one. In Cincinnati she had
come face-to-face with slavery; she had become aware of fugitives

1

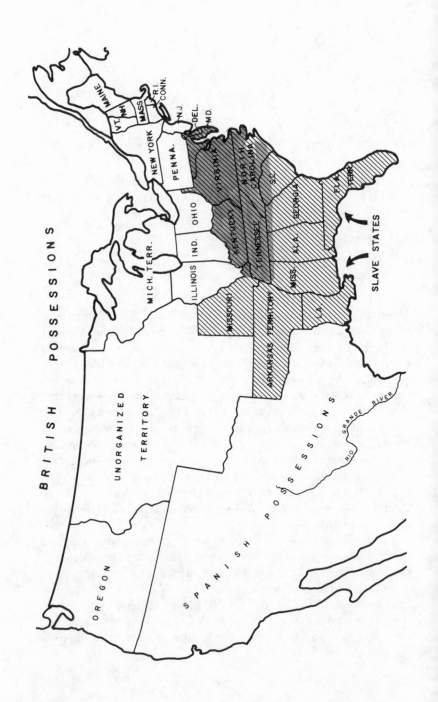

fleeing from slave states to the free soil of Ohio. In Cincinnati she had witnessed the birth of a special type of abolitionism. She had also seen in that northern city violent and shocking acts committed against those who dared to speak against slavery.

The journey east from Ohio had been an adventure for the children with her — to Pittsburgh by river steamboat and then by canalboat, and finally by train to Philadelphia. They visited their Uncle Henry Ward Beecher in Brooklyn, New York, and spent a week in Hartford, Connecticut. In Boston they paid a visit to another uncle, the Reverend Edward Beecher. Edward was an abolitionist; in fact, he had belonged to an antislavery association as early as 1825. His wife Isabella shared his views, and their home was a gathering place for people with similar sentiments. Harriet perceived their consternation at proposed legislation about fugitive slaves. This legislation did pass Congress and was the trigger that induced Harriet to write *Uncle Tom's Cabin*. We shall digress here in order to gain more familiarity with the historic background.

When Alabama entered the Union in 1819, it preserved the balance between free and slave-holding states. (There were eleven of each.) With this balance, slavery would gain no increased support in the Senate, where each state had equal representation. The North, with its greater population, had more members in the House of Representatives; but bills had to pass both houses. There was much dissention over Missouri, which had petitioned to come in as a slave state. Before the matter was settled, Maine applied to enter as a free state. So a compromise was agreed upon, allowing Missouri in as a slave state, Maine as free, and stipulating that in the future slavery could not exist in all other parts of the Louisiana Purchase north of the line 36° 30′. (This meant that slavery could be extended only into what is now Arkansas and Oklahoma. The original territory obtained from France extended from the Mississippi River to the Rocky Mountains and from the Gulf of Mexico to British North America. Louisiana and Mississippi had already been admitted as slave states.)

For 30 years this "Missouri Compromise" was in effect, but the Mexican War Treaty brought fresh problems. The United States gained the territories of New Mexico, California, and Utah. Antislavery forces were determined to curb the spread of slavery into the

Opposite: The United States after the Missouri Compromise in 1821. Courtesy Northern Michigan University, Cartographic Laboratory.

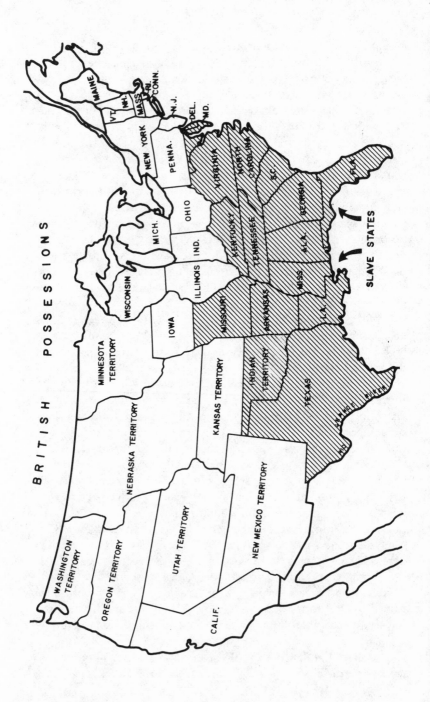

newly acquired land, but the war had been supported by those who wished to see it extended. The independent republic of Texas had been admitted as a slave state in 1845. California came in as free in 1850 and would remain so, but California's application for admission in 1849 had caused a grave crisis. Henry Clay, now old and ailing, was serving as a senator from Kentucky. Determined to preserve the Union, he was instrumental in shaping another compromise whereby the status of the New Mexico and Utah territories would be worked out when application for statehood was submitted. In addition, the slave trade in the District of Columbia would be abolished, and the fugitive slave laws of 1793 enforced throughout the nation.

A federal act of 1793 provided for the return of escaped slaves. In the free states this was largely disregarded, and by the middle of the nineteenth century, aid to fugitive slaves had become a commitment of the abolitionist movement. To appease the South, the new compromise provided for strict enforcement: "all good citizens" were to assist federal marshals and their deputies in returning fugitives to their owners. There would be no trial for an apprehended black — the word of a master claiming ownership would be final. In the case of free blacks, tragic mistakes might be made, with these legally emancipated Negroes being arrested as runaways and having no redress. Most Northerners tended to agree with the 1816 pronouncement of George Bourne, a Presbyterian minister who did not countenance slavery: "No human law must be obeyed when it contravenes the divine command."

In the biography of his mother, Charles Stowe wrote: "her soul was all on fire with indignation at this new indignity and wrong about to be inflicted by the slave-power on the innocent and helpless." But apparently Harriet listened well and said little on the subject.

The house the Stowes had arranged to rent was more than 40 years old and seems to have been in need of repairs. Henry Wadsworth Longfellow had lived there as a sophomore at Bowdoin College, but Harriet was probably less interested in its history than in getting it ready for occupancy for her family before the baby arrived. (In 1963, Stowe House was designated a Registered National Landmark.) The storm lasted for several days and delayed the arrival of

Opposite: The United States in 1850. Courtesy Northern Michigan University, Cartographic Laboratory.

the family's household effects. A friendly professor and his wife opened their home to the Stowes until the sailing ship with their goods arrived from Boston. Somehow Harriet got everything settled before the birth on July 8 of Charles Edward, who was her last child, and who, incidentally, would write her approved biography. Calvin had arrived only a few days before the birth.

According to *Crusader in Crinoline*, Harriet's biography by Forrest Wilson, Lane had not found a replacement for Calvin, and he had promised to teach there during the coming winter session. Bowdoin graciously granted him a three-month leave of absence for this; but now Andover Theological Seminary in Massachusetts offered him an attractive position as Professor of Sacred Literature. For years Calvin had failed to earn the salary he knew he was worth, and he was determined to have the Andover professorship regardless of any obligations to Lane or Bowdoin. After much discussion, Bowdoin again released him for a period to be spent at Andover during the winter of 1852. It was agreed that in the following summer he could begin full-time work at the Massachusetts institution. But meanwhile, the Stowes' financial position was as precarious as ever, and in the fall of 1850 Harriet was running a school of sorts in her home. She was also writing regularly for the *National Era*, an anti-slavery publication in Washington, D.C. Edited by the well-known abolitionist Gamaliel Bailey, the *Era*'s aim was "to mingle literature with politics." Indeed, Harriet was in good company—Whittier was an associate editor, while contributors included Hawthorne, Melville, and Lowell.

Brunswick is on the Androscoggin River, very close to the coast. Its prosperity was in part based on shipbuilding. Iron and later steel would replace wooden ships, but the sailing ships made of timber from the woods that surrounded the town were still being produced in the mid-1800s. In fact, the Stowes sometimes watched launchings. Harriet was happy to be back in her native New England. She soon became familiar with the bays, coves, and islands near Brunswick, and in time they and the Maine people would be portrayed in her writings.

Congress passed the Fugitive Slave Act in the fall of 1850. Massachusetts's Daniel Webster had backed Clay's compromise with his last eloquent oration, which began, "I speak today for the preservation of the Union. Hear me for my cause." Because this stand permitted the spread of slavery, Webster was reviled by the antislavery forces. Although the enactment was expected, the abolitionists were outraged. Isabella Beecher wrote to her literary sister-in-law: "Hattie, if I could use a pen as you can, I would write something that will make this whole nation feel what an accursed thing slavery is."

Harriet's reply was: "As long as the baby sleeps with me nights I can't do much at any thing—but I shall do it at last. I shall write that thing if I live..."

Calvin left in December for Cincinnati. Early in January, 1851, Henry Ward visited Harriet, arriving by train during a wild blizzard. The handsome brother whom she loved so dearly was becoming famous. Three years before, he had accepted a call to Plymouth Church in Brooklyn. His preaching had tremendous appeal (it has been described as spellbinding), his articles were well received by a substantial Congregational publication named the *Independent*, and he was giving lectures such as the one he had just delivered in Boston's Tremont Temple. Even the finances of his church were in good shape; so he felt himself in a position to make positive contributions to the antislavery cause. In 1848 he had held a slave "auction"—the practice of selling a slave for liberty. He would continue this at Plymouth Church, collecting the money at Sunday service, with the subject present. He knew very well that such an emotional and dramatic act would publicize the evil of slavery, besides, of course, making a free Negro of a slave. Beecher had already welcomed the able abolitionist orator, Wendell Phillips, to his pulpit, a pulpit to which the eyes of the nation were beginning to turn.

Harriet mentioned Isabella's letter and told him that she too intended to fight slavery—and by writing something. Henry encouraged her, but he was an egotist, absorbed in his own affairs, and it is likely that he regarded his sister's intention as inconsequential.

According to members of the Stowe family, some weeks later at church Harriet had a vision. She saw a Negro being flogged viciously at the order of his master. As the man died, he prayed that those who had wronged him would be forgiven. Harriet participated in the communion service in a mechanical, distracted manner, and afterwards walked home. Later that day she wrote out her vision, using names. The saint-like man was Uncle Tom, the owner was Simon Legree, and his henchmen were Sambo and Quimbo. Then she added something: the Christ-like action of Uncle Tom made converts of

Sambo and Quimbo. (Today Pew 23 of Brunswick's First Parish Church, where Harriet sat, is marked with a bronze plaque.)

Stowe family biographers contend that when Calvin returned from Ohio, he found the manuscript. It moved him to tears, and he urged his wife to use her vision as the climax to her "thing" that would condemn slavery.

On March 9 Harriet wrote to the editor of the *National Era*:

> Mr. Bailey, Dear Sir:
>
> I am at present occupied upon a story which will be much longer than any I have ever written, embracing a series of sketches which give the lights and shadows of the "patriarchal institution," written either from observation, incidents which have occurred in the sphere of my personal knowledge, or in the knowledge of my friends. I shall show the best side of the thing, and something faintly approaching the worst.
>
> Up to this year I have always felt that I had no particular call to meddle with the subject, and I dreaded to expose even my own mind to the full force of its existing power. But I feel now that the time is come when even a woman or a child who can speak for freedom and humanity is bound to speak. The Carthagenian women in the last peril of their state cut off their hair for bow-strings to give the defenders of their country; and such peril and shame as now hangs over this country is worse than Roman slavery, and I hope every woman who can write will not be silent...
>
> My vocation is simply that of a painter, and my object will be to hold up in the most lifelike and graphic manner possible Slavery, its reverses, changes, and the negro character, which I have had ample opportunities for studying. There is no arguing with pictures, and everyone is impressed by them, whether they mean to be or not.
>
> I wrote beforehand, because I know that you have much matter to arrange, and I thought it might not be amiss to give you a hint. The thing may extend through three or four numbers. It will be ready in two or three weeks....

For the projected three-or-four-part serial, Dr. Bailey was willing to pay $300, a generous sum for that day. But the work became about ten times the length anticipated, and Bailey appears to have stuck to his original price.

The *National Era* was a magazine (really more like a weekly newspaper) that came out every Thursday. On May 8 it announced a new story by Mrs. H.B. Stowe—*Uncle Tom's Cabin* or *The Man That Was a Thing*, to be published at a later date. (A serialized story or novel was not unusual; indeed, it was common for Dickens to publish in this manner.) When the first part finally appeared in the issue of June 5, the subtitle had been changed to *Life Among the Lowly*.

An unsigned letter to the editor in the July 1 issue gave hint of what was to come:

> Sir: Uncle Tom's Cabin increases in interest and pathos with each successive number. None of thy various contributions, rich and varied as they have been, have so deeply interested thy female readers of this vicinity as this story of Mrs. Stowe has so far done and promises to do.

Soon *Uncle Tom's* author was having difficulty producing the required weekly installments. In addition to all the usual demands imposed upon her by a large and active family, there was another obstacle. Her father, the distinguished Lyman Beecher, now 75, was visiting. His chief interest just then was to prepare his views on theology for publication, and to help him, he had on hand one of the stepdaughters by his third marriage. (The current Mrs. Beecher was also a visitor.) There is small likelihood that he had any idea that his daughter's publication would far outshine his, and he cannot be blamed for not realizing what would happen. Apparently Harriet wrote whenever and wherever she could, refusing to be deterred by trivial events. She often used the kitchen table as her desk. And aside from the considerable stress of having to produce, Harriet found that summer in Maine very pleasant. But there were undercurrents that she could not escape; for instance, one of the Bowdoin professors maintained that blood would be shed before the slavery problem was solved.

The installment (really a chapter) for July 24 arrived late. Most of the other material for the issue was already set up, leaving insufficient space for the complete installment. So the editor was forced to divide it, much to the author's chagrin. On August 21 a notice advised that "'Uncle Tom's Cabin' reached us at too late an hour for insertion this week. Mrs. Stowe having requested that it should not be divided, our readers may look for the entire chapter in the next *Era*."

In the issue of September 4, Dr. Bailey noted that, in answer to inquiries, *Uncle Tom* would appear in book form; that Mrs. Stowe had taken out a copyright, but the publication date and cost were not yet made public.

Harriet's oldest sister Catherine was another visitor to

Brunswick that summer. She read Harriet's work as far as it was written and was impressed. Phillips, Samson and Company of Boston had recently published her own *True Remedy of the Wrongs of Women*, and she thought they might be interested in *Uncle Tom*. So, with Harriet's permission, she approached them. However, the house had a large southern following and turned down the suggestion.

Another Boston publisher was more courageous. He was John P. Jewett, definitely antislavery and friendly with Gamaliel Bailey. In Jewett's own words, "my attention was called to this story [*Uncle Tom*] by my noble and gifted wife, to whom the entire credit is due for its publication in book form...." But this takes us ahead of the story.

Harriet's literary project was demanding more and more of her time and energy. The narrative grew and grew, with the author unwilling or unable to control it. She had little time for revision. Later she admitted that she "no more thought of style or literary excellence than the mother who rushes into the street and cries for help to save her children from a burning house thinks of the teachings of the rhetorician or the elocutionist." Catherine, if no one else, realized her sister's predicament. She agreed to spend a year in the Stowe household in order to help Harriet. Here is a portion of a letter written to her by her sister, Mary Perkins, in September, 1851: "At eight o'clock we are through with breakfast and prayers and then we send off Mr. Stowe and Harriet both to his room in the college. There is no other way to keep her out of family cares and quietly at work, and since this plan is adopted, she goes ahead finely." Calvin's "room" was in Appleton Hall. Women rarely frequented campus buildings, but now one did. Later, when Calvin went to Andover, she had the office to herself.

Sometimes Harriet shared her chapters with some of their faculty friends. Her own family was, of course, a captive audience to whom she could read each installment as she composed it. But the Stowes needed no encouragement to listen—they, like the *Era*'s readers, were impatient to know what was going to happen.

There were irate protests to the *Era* when the October 30 issue failed to carry a chapter of *Uncle Tom*. (Bear in mind that readers of that day had no television to occupy their leisure hours.) There were also protests when the magazine published the suggestion that Mrs. Stowe's long story could be finished quickly with a brief summary.

Apparently the readership not only wanted to know what happened, but also wanted to be informed in the style to which they had become accustomed. Here is a letter from one *Era* subscriber:

> Please signify to Mrs. Stowe that it will be quite agreeable to the wishes of the many readers of the <u>Era</u> for her <u>not to hurry through</u> "Uncle Tom". We don't get sleepy reading it. Having resided many years among slaves and being familiar with their habits, thoughts, feelings, and language, I have not been able to detect a single mistake in her story in any of these respects — 'tis perfect in its way — will do great good.

The issue of December 18 carried this announcement:

> We regret, as much as any of our readers can regret, that Mrs. Stowe had no chapter in this week's *Era*. It is not our fault, for up to this hour we have nothing from her. As she is generally so punctual, we fear that sickness may have prevented. We feel constrained to make this apology, so profound is the interest taken in her story by nearly all our readers.

After that, the author managed not only to keep up but to have a few installments ready in advance of the deadline. It was at the end of the fortieth "number" (the book has 44 chapters) that she wrote *finis* to the story line. With regard to length, the finished work was, of course, a far cry from what Harriet had originally proposed to Dr. Bailey.

There is considerable doubt about the exact date of the signing of the book contract. John Jewett offered 50 percent of the profits if the Stowes could pay 50 percent of the publication cost. Calvin had no money, so settled for a ten percent royalty on all sales. (As to the *Uncle Tom* plays, the first law to grant dramatic rights so as to secure a percentage on all presentations of dramatizations did not pass until 1856. Likewise, the foreign copyright act was not in effect until about 40 years later.)

The publication day was March 20, 1852. (Curiously, the last installment in the *Era* appeared on April 1.) The book consisted of two volumes with a woodcut of a cabin as the frontispiece. There were three styles of bindings: paper cover, selling at $1; cloth at $1.50; and cloth full-gilt at $2. Calvin returned to Brunswick with a supply of early copies, including some cloth full-gilt, the cloth being lavender. The original run produced 5,000 copies. Three thousand sold on the first day, and it became clear that filling orders would be a problem. Jewett got out more printings, and in three weeks 20,000 copies had sold. The *Boston Traveller* noted "three power presses running twenty-four hours a day (except Sundays), one hundred bookbinders at work, three mills running to supply the paper." By January, 1853, 200,000 copies had sold in this country, and this was only the beginning.

Harriet did not own a silk dress and had high hopes that the royalties would make it possible for her to buy a black one; she was not disappointed. She received $10,300 as her copyright premium on three months' sales of *Uncle Tom*, believed at the time to be the largest sum ever received by an American or European author from the sale of a single work in so short a period of time. The book was enormously popular in England; the *London Times* of September 3, 1852, noted that *"Uncle Tom's Cabin* is at every railway book-stall in England, and in every third traveller's hand. The book is a decided hit." (Eventually *Uncle Tom* was translated into many foreign languages.)

By April, 1852, laudatory responses were pouring in. The reviewer of the influential *Independent* wrote: "This book is full of the intensest Truth... Let ALL MEN read it!" Kudos arrived from Longfellow and Whittier. Senator Charles Sumner of Massachusetts wrote his praises, while Senator William Seward of New York claimed *Uncle Tom* as "the greatest book of all times." And so it went.

Later the people of the South woke up. The comment of the *Southern Literary Messenger* was a forerunner of the mounting conflict:

> Let it be bourne in mind that this slanderous work has found its way to every section of our country, and has crossed the water to Great Britain, filling the minds of all who know nothing of slavery with hatred for that institution and those who uphold it. Justice to ourselves would seem to demand that it should not be suffered to circulate longer without the brand of falsehood upon it.... [Mrs. Stowe deserves criticism] as the mouthpiece of a large and dangerous faction which if we do not put down with the pen, we may be compelled one day (God grant that day may never come!) to repel with the bayonet.

> October, 1852

2

A Noble Work

If you have never read it, you should.
— *Edmund Wilson*
New Yorker
November 27, 1948

We present here a somewhat detailed abstract of *Uncle Tom's Cabin*. It will serve as a review for those familiar with the book and may prompt some who do not know *Uncle Tom* to read it. To avoid personal interpretation, the author has used Mrs. Stowe's own words whenever possible.

The story opens in Kentucky, and the reader is introduced to the Shelby plantation, where the least oppressive type of slavery exists. Mr. Shelby has accumulated debts and is being forced to sell some of his slaves to a trader named Haley. The slave trader insists on having Tom, the plantation's best and trusted hand. He also wants Harry, who is an appealing quadroon aged four or five. Mr. Shelby is a weak man; he is also a kind master and against separating families. Tom has a wife, Chloe, and three young children. Besides not wishing to part with Tom, Mr. Shelby is loath to lose Harry, whose mother, Eliza is the personal maid of Mrs. Shelby. But Shelby has no choice, and he signs the necessary papers. The plot is essentially the subsequent fortunes of Tom and of Eliza and her family.

Mrs. Stowe comments:

> So long as the law considers all these human beings, with beating hearts and living affections, only as so many *things* belonging to a master, — so long as the failure, or misfortune, or imprudence, or death of the kindest owner may cause them any day to exchange a life of kind protection and indulgence for one of hopeless misery and toil, — so long it is impossible to

13

make anything beautiful or desirable in the best-regulated administration of slavery.

Here is a description of Tom, or Uncle Tom, as he is known to many on the plantation:

> He was a large, broad-chested, powerfully made man, of a full glossy black, and a face whose truly African features were characterized by an expression of grave and steady good sense, united with much kindliness and benevolence. There was something about his whole air self-respecting and dignified, yet united with a confiding and humble simplicity.

A deeply religious man, Tom studies the Bible at every opportunity. He can read a little but finds the process tedious; he prefers to listen as Mas'r George reads. George Shelby is the 13-year-old son of the family and is devoted to Uncle Tom. When the transaction with Haley becomes known, Chloe suggests that Tom try to run away, but her husband refuses. Here they are talking in their cabin:

> "Mas'r always found me on the spot, — he always will. I never have broke trust, nor used my pass no ways contrary to my word, and I never will. It's better for me alone to go, than to break up the place and sell all. Mas'r an't to blame, Chloe, and he'll take care of you and the poor" —
> Here he turned to the rough trundle-bed full of little woolly heads, and broke fairly down. He leaned over the back of the chair, and covered his face with his large hands. Sobs, heavy, hoarse, and loud, shook the chair, and great tears fell through his fingers on the floor: just such tears, sir, as you dropped into the coffin where lay your first-born son; such tears, woman, as you shed when you heard the cries of your dying babe. For, sir, he was a man, — and you are but another man. And, woman, though dressed in silk and jewels, you are but a woman, and, in life's great straits and mighty griefs ye feel but one sorrow!

Eliza is described as a beautiful quadroon, about 25, brought up by Mrs. Shelby as a petted and indulged favorite. According to Harriet:

> Eliza, such as we have described her, is not a fancy sketch, but taken from remembrance, as we saw her, years ago, in Kentucky. Safe under the protecting care of her mistress, Eliza had reached maturity without those temptations which make beauty so fatal an inheritance to a slave.

Eliza's husband is George Harris, who now comes to visit her. He is a bright and talented mulatto slave from a neighboring estate. For a time he had been hired out by his master to work in a bagging factory, where he invented a machine to clean hemp. Such independence and industry angered George's master, who ordered the proud young black slave back to the "meanest drudgery of the farm." When George's superior at the factory had remonstrated with George's owner, the latter had remarked: "It's a free country, sir, the man's *mine*, and I do what I please with him — that's it!"

Eliza is a Christian, thanks to Mrs. Shelby. George does not accept Christianity, and he is rebellious. When he complains about his abusive owner, Eliza says: "it is dreadful, but, after all, he is your master, you know."

Her husband replies:

> My master! and who made him my master? That's what I think of, — what right has he to me? I'm a man as much as he is. I'm a better man than he is. I know more about business than he does; I am a better manager than he is; I can read better than he can; I can write a better hand, — and I've learned it all myself, and no thanks to him, — I've learned it in spite of him; and now what right has he to make a drayhorse of me? — to take me from things I can do, and do better than he can...

Then George tells Eliza that he is resolved to escape to Canada or to die in the attempt. Harriet describes their parting as "such as those may make whose hope to meet again is as the spider's web."

Already worried about her husband, Eliza is devastated when she finds out about the plans for her son. Losing no time, she decides to flee to Ohio with Harry, who is asleep at the moment.

> But there, on the bed, lay her slumbering boy, his long curls falling negligently around his unconscious face, his rosy mouth half open, his little fat hands thrown over the bedclothes, and a smile spread like a sunbeam over his whole face.

Eliza quickly gathers together a few necessities and leaves with Harry. At this point, Harriet interjects:

> If it were *your* Harry, mother, or your Willie, that were going to be torn from you by a brutal trader, to-morrow morning, — if you had seen the man, and heard that the papers were signed and delivered, and you had only from twelve o'clock till morning to make good your escape, — how

Eliza comes to tell Uncle Tom that he is sold and that she is running away to save her child.   Page 62.

fast could *you* walk? How many miles could you make in those few brief hours, with the darling at your bosom, — the little sleepy head on your shoulder, — the small, soft arms trustingly holding on to your neck?

Eliza is hurrying toward the Ohio River. By daybreak she is following an open highway where she had sometimes ridden with her mistress. Now Harry is walking beside her. Will anyone suspect they are fugitives? Harriet explains:

> As she was also so white as not to be known as of colored lineage, without a critical survey, and her child was white also, it was much easier for her to pass on unsuspected.

One hour before sunset, she sees the Ohio, "which lay, like Jordan, between her and the Canaan of liberty on the other side."

> It was now early spring, and the river was swollen and turbulent; great cakes of floating ice were swinging heavily to and fro in the turbid waters. Owing to the peculiar form of the shore on the Kentucky side, the land bending far out into the water, the ice had been lodged and detained in great quantities, and the narrow channel which swept round the bend was full of ice, piled one cake over another, thus forming a temporary barrier to the descending ice, which lodged, and formed a great, undulating raft, filling up the whole river, and extending almost to the Kentucky shore.

Eliza learns that no ferry is leaving immediately, and the weary fugitives, unrecognized as such, are allowed to rest in a public house. Haley, of course, is now in pursuit. Mr. Shelby had provided him with a horse and two young slaves named Sam and Andy who know the way to the river. But these friends of Eliza had ingeniously provided a series of roadblocks that delayed Haley's arrival.

> In consequence of all the various delays, it was about three quarters of an hour after Eliza had laid her child to sleep in the village tavern that the party came riding into the same place. Eliza was standing by the window, looking out in another direction, when Sam's quick eye caught a glimpse of her. Haley and Andy were two yards behind. At this crisis, Sam contrived to have his hat blown off, and uttered a loud and characteristic ejaculation, which startled her at once; she drew suddenly back; the whole train swept by the window, round to the front door.

Opposite: Illustration from Uncle Tom's Cabin. Courtesy Library of Congress.

A thousand lives seemed to be concentrated in that one moment to Eliza. Her room opened by a side door to the river. She caught her child, and sprang down the steps towards it. The trader caught a full glimpse of her, just as she was disappearing down the bank, and throwing himself from his horse, and calling loudly on Sam and Andy, he was after her like a hound after a deer. In that dizzy moment her feet to her scarce seemed to touch the ground, and a moment brought her to the water's edge. Right on behind her they came; and, nerved with strength such as God gives only to the desperate, with one wild cry and flying leap, she vaulted sheer over the turbid current by the shore, on to the raft of ice beyond. It was a desperate leap, —impossible to anything but madness and despair; and Haley, Sam, and Andy instinctively cried out, and lifted up their hands, as she did it.

The huge green fragment of ice on which she alighted pitched and creaked as her weight came on it, but she stayed there not a moment. With wild cries and desperate energy she leaped to another and still another cake; —stumbling, —leaping, —slipping, —springing upwards again! Her shoes are gone, —her stockings cut from her feet, —while blood marked every step; but she saw nothing, felt nothing, till dimly, as in a dream, she saw the Ohio side, and a man helping her up the bank.

Back at the tavern on the Kentucky side, the downcast Haley encounters an acquaintance named Tom Loker. Loker and his companion, Marks, are slave catchers. Haley's description of Eliza interests them, and they decide to pursue her; their plan is to sell her themselves. They make a deal to return little Harry to Haley, now the legal owner of the child.

On the Ohio side, Eliza is helped up the bank by a farmer who lives near the Shelbys. He recognizes her but admires her courage and thinks she has earned her freedom. So instead of returning her to her owners, he directs her to a large white house where he knows she will find sanctuary. Harriet sarcastically describes the man as a

poor, heathenish Kentuckian, who had not been instructed in his constitutional relations, and consequently was betrayed into acting in a sort of Christianized manner, which, if he had been better situated and more enlightened, he would not have been left to do.

The owner of the white house is Senator John Bird of the Ohio state legislature. He and Mrs. Bird are discussing a recently passed law that forbids giving aid to fugitive slaves. The senator says he would uphold the law, though he regards doing so a painful duty. His wife is not convinced. Law, or no law, she says, she would never turn away from her door a poor, fleeing slave, and she tells her husband that he wouldn't either. Her contention is about to be tested, for the desperate Eliza and her boy are now warming up in the senator's kitchen, aided and comforted by Aunt Dinah and old Cudjoe, free blacks in the employ of the Birds. Mrs. Bird is as good as her word:

> With many gentle and womanly offices which none knew better how to render than Mrs. Bird, the poor woman was, in time, rendered more calm. A temporary bed was provided for her on the settle, near the fire; and, after a short time, she fell into a heavy slumber, with the child, who seemed no less weary, soundly sleeping on her arm; for the mother resisted, with nervous anxiety, the kindest attempts to take him from her; and, even in sleep, her arm encircled him with an unrelaxing clasp, as if she could not even then be beguiled of her vigilant hold.

Later in the evening when Eliza tells the assembled household that she jumped over the ice floes to save her son, Mrs. Bird bursts into tears; she herself had buried a child a month ago. Eliza says to her:

> Then you will feel for me. I have lost two, one after another, — left 'em buried there when I came away; and I had only this one left. I never slept a night without him; he was all I had. He was my comfort and pride, day and night; and, ma'am, they were going to take him away from me, — to *sell* him, — sell him down south, ma'am, to go all alone, — a baby that had never been away from his mother in his life! I couldn't stand it, ma'am. I knew I never should be good for anything, if they did; and when I knew the papers were signed, and he was sold, I took him and came off in the night; and they chased me....

Of course Mrs. Bird has judged her husband correctly, and he makes plans to transport the fugitives to a remote place seven miles up the creek. By midnight Cudjoe and the senator have Eliza and Harry in a carriage that bounces and jounces over an Ohio corduroy road "where the mud is of unfathomable and sublime depth." And there was danger in crossing the swollen creek. Harriet interjects:

> What a situation, now, for a patriotic senator, that had been all the week before spurring up the legislature of his native state to pass more stringent resolutions against escaping fugitives, their harborers and abettors!...
> He was as bold as a lion about it, and "mightily convinced" not only himself, but everybody that heard him; — but then his idea of a fugitive was only an idea of the letters that spell the word, — or, at the most, the image

of a little newspaper picture of a man with a stick and bundle, with "Ran away from the subscriber" under it. The magic of the real presence of distress, — the imploring human eye, the frail, trembling human hand, the despairing appeal of helpless agony, — these he had never tried. He had never thought that a fugitive might be a hapless mother, a defenceless child, — like that one which was now wearing his lost boy's little well-known cap; and so, as our poor senator was not stone or steel, — as he was a man, and a downright noblehearted one, too, — he was, as everybody must see, in a sad case for his patriotism.

Finally the stormy ride is over, and the mother and son are safe under the roof of John Van Trompe, ex-slaveowner from Kentucky, who is now associated with the Underground. Senator Bird drives to the next tavern to catch the stage to Columbus. This should satisfy any who might wonder why his carriage is out until dawn.

Now back to Uncle Tom's cabin. It is, at best, a dismal morning, for today Tom will leave his family. Chloe is getting his things together and has prepared a last meal of her husband's favorite foods, but she cannot keep back the tears. "I'm in the Lord's hands," declares Tom, but his wife feels differently.

> 't an't right! 't an't right it should be so! Mas'r never ought ter left it so that ye *could* be took for his debts. Ye 've arnt him all he gets for ye, twice over. He owed ye yer freedom, and ought ter gin't to yer years ago. Mebbe he can't help himself now, but I feel it's wrong. Nothing can't beat that ar out o' me. Sich a faithful crittur as ye 've been, — and allers sot his business 'fore yer own every way, — and reckon on him more than yer own wife and chil'en!

The boys are whimpering as Tom, for the last time, plays with the baby on his knee. Chloe cries:

> ye'll have to come to it, too! ye'll live to see yer husband sold, or mebbe be sold yerself; and these yer boys, they's to be sold, I s'pose, too, jest like as not, when dey gets good for somethin'; an't no use in niggers havin' nothin'!

In sight of all the assembled servants, Haley takes Tom away in a wagon. He fastens Tom's ankles in shackles. Mrs. Shelby protests, for she knows that Tom's word can be trusted, but Haley pays no attention. After about a mile's ride, Haley stops at a blacksmith's shop to have a pair of handcuffs made large enough for Tom.

At this point, young George Shelby rides up. He has been away visiting and has just learned of Tom's plight. He throws his arms around the black and voices fury at Tom's sale. To Haley he says, "I should think you'd be ashamed to spend all your life buying men and women, chaining them, like cattle! I should think you'd feel mean!"

Haley returns, "So long as grand folks wants to buy men and women, I'm as good as they is; 'tan't any meaner sellin' on 'em, than 'tis buyin'!"

George replies to this, "I'll never do either, when I'm a man. I'm ashamed this day that I'm a Kentuckian. I was always proud of it before." He has a silver dollar with a hole in it for a string. This he hands round Tom's neck, cautioning him to keep it hidden from sight. It is a reminder to Tom that his young massa intends to find someday a way to return the beloved slave to the Shelbys.

Now the reader moves back to a small Kentucky hotel where there is posted a handbill that describes George Harris, the husband of Eliza:

> Ran away from the subscriber, my mulatto boy, George. Said George six feet in height, a very light mulatto, brown curly hair; is very intelligent, speaks handsomely, can read and write; will probably try to pass for a white man; is deeply scarred on his back and shoulders; has been branded in his right hand with the letter H.
>
> I will give four hundred dollars for him alive, and the same sum for satisfactory proof that he has been killed.

Among those in the barroom is a man named Wilson who lets it drop that the George described in the advertisement had worked for several years in Wilson's bagging factory; the slave had even invented a machine to clean hemp, to which George's master now holds the patent. A stranger now arrives at the inn, driven there in a one-horse buggy by a black attendant. The newcomer is tall and dark, of perhaps Spanish descent; he identifies himself as Henry Butler. When Wilson introduces himself, Butler contrives to see him alone, and it soon becomes clear that Butler is really George Harris.

Wilson realizes the unfairness and the harshness of George's lot, but feels dutybound to discourage his former employee to seek his freedom:

> Yes, my boy, I'm sorry for you, now; it's a bad case, — very bad; but the apostle says, Let every one abide in the condition in which he is called. We must all submit to the inclinations of Providence, George, — don't you see?

George returns:

> I wonder, Mr. Wilson, if the Indians should come and take you a prisoner away from your wife and children, and want to keep you all your life hoeing corn for them, if you'd think it your duty to abide in the condition in which you were called. I rather think that you'd think the first stray horse you could find an indication of Providence, — shouldn't you?

Mr. Wilson is convinced that George means to escape to Canada to avoid the fate of a sister, who was sent to market in New Orleans. The older man urges him to trust in the Lord. The slave answers:

> Is there a God to trust in? Oh, I've seen things all my life that have made me feel that there can't be a God. You Christians don't know how these things look to us. There's a God for you, but is there any for us?

The scene now switches to Tom as he journeys with Haley. The dealer has bought three additional slaves, and owner and his chattels are now on the lower deck of a steamboat bound downstream on the Ohio. At one stop, Haley goes ashore and returns with a black woman and her ten-month-old baby. Later Tom overhears that the woman's master had tricked her into thinking that she was going to Louisville to hire out as a cook in the hotel where her husband works; in reality, she has been sold to Haley, who intends her for a plantation order he is filling. This, of course, is devastating news for her. A stranger on board notices the vitality of the baby and persuades Haley to part with him for $45. They will take the child when the mother is not watching him. At Louisville the woman moves close to the rail, hoping to catch a glimpse of her husband among the hotel waiters on the dock. When the boat casts off, she returns to a pile of boxes where she had improvised a cradle for her sleeping babe. He is gone.

Haley explains to the bewildered woman, "Your child's gone; you may as well know it first as last. You see, I know'd you couldn't take him down South; and I got a chance to sell him to a first-rate family that'll raise him better than you can." Harriet comments:

> The trader had arrived at that stage of Christian and political perfection which has been recommended by some preachers and politicians of the north, lately, in which he had completely overcome every humane weakness and prejudice. His heart was exactly where yours, sir, and mine could

be brought, with proper effort and cultivation. The wild look of anguish and utter despair that the woman cast on him might have disturbed one less practised; but he was used to it. He had seen that same look hundreds of times. You can get used to such things, too, my friend; and it is the great object of recent efforts to make our whole northern community used to them, for the glory of the Union.

Tom sees the whole despicable incident, including Haley's signal to the stranger to take the child when the mother is absent, with the hope of preventing a scene.

> His very soul bled within him for what seemed to him the *wrongs* of the poor suffering thing that lay like a crushed reed on the boxes; the feeling, living, bleeding, yet immortal *thing*, which American state law cooly classes with the bundles, and bales, and boxes, among which she is lying.

With tears running down his cheeks, he tries to comfort her, speaking of a pitying Jesus. But the disconsolate woman was incapable of listening. At midnight Tom wakes with a sudden start. He hears a splash in the water, and then he notices that the woman is gone. In the morning, Haley records the suicide by listing it in his account book under "LOSSES."

Now, for a brief space, the reader is returned to Eliza and little Harry. They have got as far as Indiana and are at the home of a Quaker family named Halliday. No fugitive slave has ever been captured in their village, but Eliza lives in constant dread and is anxious to reach Canada as soon as possible. A wagon has brought to the settlement three escaping slaves, an old woman and two men. One of the latter turns out to be George Harris, and for him there is a joyous reunion with his wife and child. When George eats breakfast with the Halliday family, it is the first time that he has sat down on equal terms at any white man's table. Simeon Halliday warns him that he is being pursued; under the cover of darkness the fugitives will be moved to the next stand.

Meanwhile, the boat carrying Tom farther and farther from his family has reached the Mississippi. She is now loaded with cotton bales, and Tom sees on the shores plantation after plantation, cypresses, and canebrakes — very different from Kentucky.

Among the passengers is a little white girl of about six. She charms everyone, including Tom. Her name is Evangeline St. Clare, and she is known as Eva. Just as the boat is leaving a landing place

where wood was taken on, Eva falls overboard and is rescued by
Tom. The next day, as the vessel approaches New Orleans, Eva's
father, on her persuasion, buys Tom from Haley for $1,300.

Augustine St. Clare, Tom's new master, is young, gay, im-
practical, and skeptical. His wife Marie is selfish and egotistical and
suffers from a variety of imaginary conditions. Their marriage is not
a happy one, and most of Augustine's love is showered on Eva. Due
to Marie's hypochondriac condition, the St. Clare home is in a state
of chaos. While visiting in Vermont with Eva, Augustine had persuaded his cousin, Miss Ophelia St. Clare, to return with them to
New Orleans. Knowing her propensity for getting things done, he
hopes she can produce some semblance of order in the St. Clare
household. Thus Miss Ophelia, as she is called, is aboard the river
steamboat too.

Augustine, Eva, Ophelia, and the newly acquired Tom arrive at
the stately St. Clare mansion and are greeted by the languid Marie
and the house servants, who, of course, are slaves. Miss Ophelia
knows nothing about Negroes, but is is clear that supervision is
needed. Augustine's father was a rich planter and Marie is an heiress,
so Augustine does not work for a living. He is kind and considerate
to his slaves almost to the point of indulgence. But he is also too lazy
to take a firm hand in the running of his affairs. Marie is an unfeeling
and demanding mistress. Night after night she keeps Mammy up
attending to her petty wants, and then complains that the woman
does not wake her up on time the next day. Mammy, by the way, has
a husband and two children who belong to Marie's father and live far
away. Here is a conversation between Marie and Miss Ophelia
about the slaves in the St. Clare mansion:

> "[St. Clare] talks the strangest stuff. He says we have made them what they
> are, and ought to bear with them. He says their faults are all owing to us,
> and that it would be cruel to make the fault and punish it too. He says we
> shouldn't do any better, in their place; just as if one could reason from
> them to us, you know."
>
> "Don't you believe that the Lord made them of one blood with us?" said
> Miss Ophelia, shortly.
>
> "No, indeed, not I! A pretty story, truly! They are a degraded race."
>
> "Don't you think they've got immortal souls?" said Miss Ophelia, with
> increasing indignation.
>
> "Oh, well," said Marie, yawning, "that, of course—nobody doubts that.
> But as to putting them on any sort of equality with us, you know, as if we
> could be compared, why, it's impossible! Now, St. Clare really has talked

to me as if keeping Mammy from her husband was like keeping me from mine. There's no comparing in this way. Mammy couldn't have the feelings that I should. It's a different thing altogether, — of course, it is, — and yet St. Clare pretends not to see it. And just as if Mammy could love her little dirty babies as I love Eva! Yet St. Clare once really and soberly tried to persuade me that it was my duty, with my weak health, and all I suffer, to let Mammy go back, and take somebody else in her place."

Tom is to be Marie's driver, replacing a drunken one. It is an easy job in beautiful surroundings. Here is a scene that involves him and Eva:

There sat Tom, on a little mossy seat in the court, every one of his button-holes stuck full of cape jessamines, and Eva, gayly laughing, was hanging a wreath of roses round his neck; and then she sat down on his knee, like a chip-sparrow, still laughing.

"Oh, Tom, you look so funny!"

Tom had a sober, benevolent smile, and seemed, in his quiet way, to be enjoying the fun quite as much as his little mistress.

When Miss Ophelia, already aghast at having seen Eva embrace Mammy, refers to the child's sitting on Uncle Tom's knee, St. Clare responds:

You would think no harm in a child's caressing a large dog, even if he was black; but a creature that can think, and reason, and feel, and is immortal, you shudder at; confess it, cousin. I know the feeling among some of you northerners well enough. Not that there is a particle of virtue in our not having it; but custom with us does what Christianity ought to do, — obliterates the feeling of personal prejudice. I have often noticed, in my travels north, how much stronger this was with you than with us. You loathe them as you would a snake or a toad, yet you are indignant at their wrongs. You would not have them abused; but you don't want to have anything to do with them yourselves. You would send them to Africa, out of your sight and smell, and then send a missionary or two to do up all the self-denial of elevating them compendiously. Isn't that it?

The Harrises now demand the reader's attention. A stalwart Quaker named Phineas Fletcher is their driver, and in the wagon with them is another Negro fugitive, Jim Selden, and his aged mother. Around 3 A.M., Phineas is warned by a cohort called Michael that they are being followed, and the horses are lashed to a run. But the slave catchers gain steadily; by dawn they are close enough to see the wagon. Phineas drives near a ledge of a steep overhanging rock that promises shelter. He orders the passengers to run up into the rocks with him, and Michael fastens his horse's bridle to the wagon and drives it ahead, seeking help.

The pursuers turn out to be, predictably, Loker and Marks, accompanied by two constables with warrants and a drunken posse of rowdies from a tavern. As they try to follow Phineas's party up the rocks, they find that at one place it is necessary to walk single file between two rocks, in range of the pistols of George and Jim. (Phineas, a Friend, is unarmed). George places himself in view of the slave catchers and declares he will fight. Harriet interjects:

> If it had been only a Hungarian youth, now, bravely defending in some mountain fastness the retreat of fugitives escaping from Austria into America, this would have been sublime heroism; but as it was a youth of African descent, defending the retreat of fugitives through America into Canada, of course we are too well instructed and patriotic to see any heroism in it; and if any of our readers do, they must do it on their own private responsibility. When despairing Hungarian fugitives make their way, against all the search-warrants and authorities of their lawful government, to America, press and political cabinet ring with applause and welcome. When despairing African fugitives do the same thing, — it is — what *is* it?*

Marks fires at George but misses. Then Loker starts up, followed by the others. He is stopped by George's bullet in his side. Alive, he falls into a chasm, while Marks leads a retreat. Afraid of confronting George again, the posse gives up and rides away, leaving behind the bleeding Tom Loker. Michael returns with help, and Loker is brought by wagon to a farmhouse where he is given good care.

The St. Clare *ménage* now dominates the scene. Tom has convinced his new master of his ability and trustworthiness and is in charge of the marketing for the household. St. Clare's failure to attend church and his propensity for imbibing freely cause distress to Tom, who prays for his master. And when an opportunity arises, he actually persuades St. Clare to stop drinking.

Miss Ophelia begins to reform the household by reprimanding Dinah, the head cook, about the lack of order in her kitchen. Here she is in action:

*The year 1848 had seen revolutions of the workers in various European countries, including Hungary. Later the Hungarian leader and hero, Lajos Kossuth, had visited the United States and had been received as a champion of liberty.

"What is this drawer for, Dinah?" she said.

"It's handy for most anything, Missis," said Dinah. So it appeared to be. From the variety it contained, Miss Ophelia pulled out first a fine damask table-cloth stained with blood, having evidently been used to envelop some raw meat.

"What's this, Dinah? You don't wrap up meat in your mistress's best table-cloths?"

"Oh Lor, Missis, no; the towels was all a missin', — so I jest did it. I laid out to wash that ar, — that's why I put it thar."

"Shif'less!" said Miss Ophelia to herself, proceeding to tumble over the drawer, where she found a nutmeg-grater and two or three nutmegs, a Methodist hymn-book, a couple of soiled Madras handkerchiefs, some yarn and knitting-work, a paper of tobacco and a pipe, a few crackers, one or two gilded china saucers with some pomade in them, one or two thin old shoes, a piece of flannel carefully pinned up enclosing some white onions, several damask table-napkins, some coarse crash towels, some twine and darning-needles, and several broken papers, from which sundry sweet herbs were sifting into the drawer.

Later, when the exasperated Miss Ophelia relates her findings to her cousin, this conversation follows:

[Augustine] "Don't I know that the rolling-pin is under her bed, and the nutmeg-grater in her pocket with her tobacco, — that there are sixty-five different sugar-bowls, one in every hole in the house, — that she washes dishes with a dinner-napkin one day, and with a fragment of an old petti-coat the next? But the upshot is, she gets up glorious dinners, makes superb coffee; and you must judge her as warriors and statesmen are judged, by *her success*."

[Miss Ophelia] "I can't help feeling as if these servants were not *strictly honest*. Are you sure they can be relied on?"

[Augustine] "Well, now and then one, whom nature makes so impracti-cably simple, truthful, and faithful, that the worst possible influence can't destroy it. But, you see, from the mother's breast the colored child feels and sees that there are none but underhand ways open to it. It can get along no other way with its parents, its mistress, its young master and missie play-fellows. Cunning and deception become necessary, inevitable habits. It isn't fair to expect anything else of him. He ought not to be punished for it. As to honesty, the slave is kept in that dependent, semi-childish state, that there is no making him realize the rights of property, or feel that his master's goods are not his own, if he can get them. For my part, I don't see how they *can* be honest. Such a fellow as Tom, here, is — is a moral miracle!"

The good lady gains more insight into the tragedy of slavery when she hears about old Prue, the Negress who sells rusks and hot

rolls to the St. Clares. Prue's former master bought her to breed
children for market—children lost forever to her when they were
sold. Her present master is not a speculator, so she had had high
hopes of keeping her last baby. But when she got sick, she lost her
milk, and her mistress refused to buy milk for the infant. The baby's
crying annoyed the mistress, and Prue was forced to put her child in
a garret while she herself slept in the mistress's room. After the babe
died in the garret, Prue turned to alcohol to blot out her anguish.
When Miss Ophelia learns one day that Prue has been whipped to
death because she was drunk again, the spinster from New England is
aghast. She addresses her cousin. "Haven't you got any selectmen,
or anybody, to interfere and look after such matters?" He replies:

> It's commonly supposed that the *property* interest is a sufficient guard in
> these cases. If people choose to ruin their own possessions, I don't know
> what's to be done. It seems the poor creature was a thief and a drunkard;
> and so there won't be much hope to get up sympathy for her....
>   If low-minded, brutal people will act like themselves, what am I to do?
> They have absolute control; they are irresponsible despots. There would
> be no use in interfering; there is no law that amounts to anything practi-
> cally, for such a case.

Augustine makes clear his abhorrence of chattel slavery. Here
are some of his thoughts:

> When I have been travelling up and down on our boats, or about on my
> collecting tours, and reflected that every brutal, disgusting, mean, low-
> lived fellow I met, was allowed by our laws to become absolute despot of
> as many men, women, and children, as he could cheat, steal, or gamble
> money enough to buy, —when I have seen such men in actual ownership of
> helpless children, of young girls and women, I have been ready to curse my
> country, to curse the human race!
>   Tell me that any man living wants to work all his days, from day-dawn
> till dark, under the constant eye of a master, without the power of putting
> forth one irresponsible volition, on the same dreary, monotonous, un-
> changing toil, and all for two pairs of pantaloons and a pair of shoes a year,
> with enough food and shelter to keep him in working order! Any man who
> thinks that human beings can, as a general thing, be made about as com-
> fortable that way as any other, I wish he might try it.

Now on stage is a nine-year-old slave child known as Topsy,
purchased by Augustine for Miss Ophelia to educate and train, but
wiley beyond her years. Harriet compares Eva and Topsy:

There stood the two children, representatives of the two extremes of society. The fair, high-bred child, with her golden head, her deep eyes, her spiritual, noble brow, and prince-like movements; and her black, keen, subtle, cringing, yet acute neighbor. They stood the representatives of their races. The Saxon, born of ages of cultivation, command, education, physical and moral eminence; the Afric, born of ages of oppression, submission, ignorance, toil, and vice!

It is soon apparent that Topsy learns quickly when she chooses to do so. She also is droll, with a vivid imagination and a flair for entertaining others. The question is, will the New England spinster be able to turn this spirited child into the sedate and God-fearing person Miss Ophelia believes Topsy should become?

The Shelbys, Tom's former owners, are now in the fore. Chloe has had a letter from Tom (written with St. Clare's help), and through it the Shelbys know that Tom has inquired when money for his redemption will be forthcoming. The family's finances have not improved, so Chloe, at her own request, hires out for $4 a week to a bakery in Louisville, with the understanding that the money she earns will repurchase Tom. Sally, her oldest, becomes the plantation's cook and also supervises the other children of Tom and Chloe. Young George Shelby relays this information to Tom.

By now the St. Clares are spending the summer at their villa on Lake Pontchartrain. The bond between Eva and Tom has grown, and she even tells him she knows that she is soon going to Heaven. This gives him a jolt; nevertheless, he has noticed that she is becoming thinner and that nothing cures her coughing; he realizes that she has a fever.

Topsy continues untamed, doing as she pleases. Her callous indifference causes much pain to Aunt Ophelia. When Eva suggests that Miss Ophelia would love Topsy if she were good, Topsy protests, "No; she can't bar me, 'cause I'm a nigger! — she'd soon have a toad touch her! There can't nobody love niggers, and niggers can't do nothin'! I don't care." The New Englander tells her cousin:

"I've always had a prejudice against Negroes, ... and it's a fact, I never could bear to have that child touch me; but I didn't think she knew it."

"Trust any child to find that out," said St. Clare; "there's no keeping it from them. But I believe that all the trying in the world to benefit a child, and all the substantial favors you can do them, will never excite one emotion of gratitude, while that feeling of repugnance remains in the heart; — it's a queer kind of a fact, — but so it is."

As Eva becomes weaker and weaker, it is Tom who carries her from place to place and sings to her their favorite hymns. It is also he who knows most of the child's imaginings and foreshadowings. Harriet writes many words about the process of the child's dying. Here is her description of a scene where Topsy offers a half-blown tea rose-bud, just after her idol has died:

> Topsy came forward and laid her offering at the feet of the corpse; then suddenly, with a wild and bitter cry, she threw herself on the floor alongside the bed, and wept, and moaned aloud.
>
> Miss Ophelia hastened into the room, and tried to raise and silence her; but in vain.
>
> "Oh, Miss Eva! Oh, Miss Eva! I wish I's dead, too, —I do!"
>
> There was a piercing wildness in the cry; the blood flushed into St. Clare's white, marble-like face, and the first tears he had shed since Eva died stood in his eyes.
>
> "Get up, child," said Miss Ophelia, in a softened voice; "don't cry so. Miss Eva is gone to heaven; she is an angel."
>
> "But I can't see her!" said Topsy. "I never shall see her!" and she sobbed again.
>
> They all stood a moment in silence.
>
> "*She* said she *loved* me," said Topsy, —"she did! Oh, dear! Oh, dear! there an't *nobody* left now, —there an't!"
>
> "That's true enough," said St. Clare; "but do," he said to Miss Ophelia, "see if you can't comfort the poor creature."
>
> "I jist wish I hadn't never been born," said Topsy." "I didn't want to be born, no ways; and I don't see no use on't."
>
> Miss Ophelia raised her gently, but firmly, and took her from the room; but, as she did so, some tears fell from her eyes.
>
> "Topsy, you poor child," she said, as she led her into her room, "don't give up! *I* can love you, though I am not like that dear little child. I hope I've learnt something of the love of Christ from her. I can love you; I do, and I'll try to help you to grow up a good Christian girl."
>
> Miss Ophelia's voice was more than her words, and more than that were the honest tears that fell down her face. From that hour, she acquired an influence over the mind of the destitute child that she never lost.

After the funeral, the St. Clares return to New Orleans. Tom in particular senses Augustine's overwhelming grief and tries to help his master find solace through faith. St. Clare is appreciative of Tom's good qualities and has begun the legal formalities of freeing the faithful slave. At the same time, his cousin insists that Topsy become hers by law because "You may die, or fail, and then Topsy be hustled off to auction, spite of all I can do." Augustine obligingly writes the necessary deed of gift. Later Miss Ophelia inquires if he has made any provision for the other servants, in case of his death. He intends to, he says, and chides her for making post-mortem arrangements with such zeal. He would like to see the South abolish slavery:

> But, suppose we should rise up to-morrow and emancipate, who would educate these millions, and teach them how to use their freedom? They never would rise to do much among us. The fact is, we are too lazy and unpractical, ourselves, ever to give them much of an idea of that industry and energy which is necessary to form them into men. They will have to go north, where labor is the fashion, — the universal custom; and tell me, now, is there enough Christian philanthropy, among your Northern States, to bear with the process of their education and elevation? You send thousands of dollars to foreign missions; but could you endure to have the heathen sent into your towns and villages, and give your time, and thoughts, and money, to raise them to the Christian standard? That's what I want to know....
>
> We are in a bad position. We are the more *obvious* oppressors of the Negro; but the unchristian prejudice of the north is an oppressor almost equally severe.

Any good intentions of Augustine come to naught, because shortly afterwards he is fatally stabbed while trying to separate two men involved in a drunken brawl. As life ebbs from him, he asks Tom to pray. Then he reaches for Tom's hand "for, in the gates of eternity, the black hand and the white hold each other with an equal clasp." Harriet digresses from the story to mention how an owner's death may disrupt a slave household:

> We hear often of the distress of the Negro servants on the loss of a kind master; and with good reason, for no creature on God's earth is left more utterly unprotected and desolate than the slave in these circumstances.
>
> The child who has lost a father has still the protection of friends, and of the law; he is something, and can do something, — has acknowledged rights and position; the slave has none. The law regards him, in every respect, as devoid of rights as a bale of merchandise. The only possible acknowledgment of any of the longings and wants of a human and immortal creature, which are given to him, comes to him through the sovereign and irresponsible will of his master; and when that master is stricken down, nothing remains.
>
> The number of those men who know how to use wholly irresponsible power humanely and generously is small. Everybody knows this, and the slave knows it best of all; so that he feels that there are ten chances of his finding an abusive and tyrannical master, to one of his finding a consider-

ate and kind one. Therefore is it that the wail over a kind master is loud
and long, as well it may be.

Marie does not believe in indulging the slaves of her household.
She begins to assert herself by sending a quadroon named Rosa to a
whipping house for 15 lashes. When it is known that the servants and
furniture are to be auctioned off, Ophelia reminds Marie that
Augustine had promised Tom his liberty and had begun the proper
legal procedure. She also brings up the fact that Eva, on her death
bed, had been assured that Tom could go free. When Ophelia sees
that nothing will move the inhumane Marie, she writes Mrs. Shelby
about Tom's plight. The next day Tom and several other servants are
sent to a slave warehouse.

The reader learns that the slave warehouse is kept clean and neat
"so as not to shock the eyes and senses of respectable society."
Likewise, "human property is high in the market; and is, therefore,
well fed, well cleaned, tended, and looked after, that it may come to
sale sleek, and strong, and shining." The buyer

> shall be courteously entreated to call and examine, and shall find an abund-
> ance of husbands, wives, brothers, sisters, fathers, mothers, and young
> children, to be "sold separately, or in lots, to suit the convenience of the
> purchaser;" and that soul immortal, once bought with blood and anguish
> by the Son of God, when the earth shook, and the rocks were rent, and the
> graves were opened, can be sold, leased, mortgaged, exchanged for grocer-
> ies or dry goods, to suit the phases of trade, or the fancy of the purchaser.

Among those for sale are a mother and daughter named Susan
and Emmeline. The 15-year-old Emmeline is a quadroon, and her
mother is tormented about her future:

> for she knows that to-morrow any man, however vile and brutal, however
> godless and merciless, if he only has money to pay for her, may become
> owner of her daughter, body and soul; and then, how is the child to be
> faithful? She thinks of all this, as she holds her daughter in her arms, and
> wishes that she were not handsome and attractive.

Susan is sold to a respectable and apparently benevolent man,
but he cannot afford her daughter. Emmeline and Tom go to a bullet-
headed, dirty man of great strength who is the owner of a cotton
plantation on the Red River. His name is Simon Legree; he has
purchased six other slaves, and the party now takes a steamer up the

Red River. Disembarking at a small town, the group finishes the journey, some traveling by wagon and some on foot.

Legree's house is in a wild, remote spot. He keeps ferocious bulldogs to track those who attempt to escape. He also has two black overseers, Sambo and Quimbo, whom he has systematically trained to be tyrannical and brutal. Tom is utterly dejected when he sees the slave quarters. There is no furniture — only a heap of filthy straw to lie on, if no one else is using it. He also finds that the hands are poorly fed and kept in rags.

There is now a huge cotton crop to be picked, and the slaves are in the fields from dawn until late in the evening, driven by the lash to the limits of endurance. When they return home, the small allotment of hard corn that constitutes supper is yet to be ground into meal in handmills. These are too few in number, with the result that the strongest Negroes always finish first because they are able to drive away the weaker ones. Tom waits his turn for a long time, and then grinds corn for two women who are exhausted from the day's work. He coaxes along a fire used by others who had done their grinding earlier. The women, in turn, mix his cake and cook it for him. Disconsolate, he tries to find comfort in reading his Bible.

One of the slaves who was purchased with Tom is a mulatto named Lucy. She cannot keep up in picking, and one day Tom helps her reach her quota by putting cotton from his basket into hers. In this he is abetted by Cassy, a proud and beautiful quadroon whom Legree has been holding as his mistress. But Sambo informs on them, and Legree orders Tom to flog Lucy. Tom says:

> "the poor crittur's sick and feeble; 't would be downright cruel, and it's what I never will do, nor begin to. Mas'r, if you mean to kill me, kill me; but, as to my raising my hand agin any one here, I never shall, — I'll die first!"
>
> "An't I yer master? Didn't I pay down twelve hundred dollars, cash, for all there is inside yer old cussed black shell? An't yer mine, now, body and soul?" he said, giving Tom a violent kick with his heavy boot, "tell me!"
>
> In the very depth of physical suffering, bowed by brutal oppression, this question shot a gleam of joy and triumph through Tom's soul. He suddenly stretched himself up, and, looking earnestly to heaven, while the tears and blood that flowed down his face mingled, he exclaimed, —
>
> "No! no! no! my soul an't yours, Mas'r! You haven't bought it, — ye can't buy it! It's been bought and paid for, by one that is able to keep it; — no matter, no matter, you can't harm me!"
>
> "I can't!" said Legree, with a sneer; "we'll see, — we'll see! Here, Sambo, Quimbo, give this dog such a breakin' in as he won't get over, this month!"

The two gigantic Negroes that now laid hold of Tom, with fiendish exultation in their faces, might have formed no unapt personification of the powers of darkness. The poor woman screamed with apprehension, and all rose, as by a general impulse, while they dragged him unresisting from the place.

Late that evening Cassy finds Tom, who has been left in a dilapidated room in the gin-house. He is bruised and bleeding and tormented by swarms of mosquitoes. Cassy gets him water and makes him as comfortable as possible. She reads the Bible to him, as he requests. During the course of her visit, he learns that 15-year-old Emmeline is now the favored of Legree. She also tells Tom her own story.

Cassy is the daughter of a black woman slave and a white owner. She was brought up in comfort and educated in a convent until she was 14. When her father died suddenly from cholera, she was sold for $2,000 to a young man she called Henry. She loved this man very much and by him had a boy, another Henry, and a girl named Elsie. For seven years they had a happy home life. Then Henry's cousin Butler encouraged him to gamble, and soon Henry had serious debts. Butler also introduced him to a woman who supplanted Cassy. Henry was forced to sell Cassy and the children to Butler. Butler in time sold Henry and Elsie to different owners, and finally Cassy was sold to a Captain Stuart, who treated her kindly. Cassy continued:

In the course of a year, I had a son born. Oh, that child! — how I loved it! How just like my poor Henry the little thing looked! But I had made up my mind, — yes, I had. I would never again let a child live to grow up! I took the little fellow in my arms, when he was two weeks old, and kissed him, and cried over him; and then I gave him laudanum, and held him close to my bosom, while he slept to death. How I mourned and cried over it! and who ever dreamed that it was anything but a mistake, that had made me give it the laudanum? but it's one of the few things that I'm glad of now. I am not sorry, to this day; he, at least, is out of pain. What better than death could I give him, poor child! After a while, the cholera came, and Captain Stuart died; everybody died that wanted to live, — and I, — I, though I went down to death's door, — *I lived!* Then I was sold, and passed from hand to hand, till I grew faded and wrinkled, and I had a fever; and then this wretch bought me, and brought me here, — and here I am!"

Despite his pain and anguish, Tom tries to soothe her sorrow and bitterness. He wants her to turn to Christ. But she says He is not there: "There's nothing here, but sin and long, long, long despair!"

Now Harriet brings Simon Legree into focus. He is the only son of a gentle and pious New England woman and a hard-hearted man. Unfortunately his mother's example had little effect, and at an early age he left home to go to sea. By the time he enters the story, he is a cruel, hard-drinking, coarse individual with little to redeem him. He is very disturbed when Sambo brings him a small paper package taken from Tom. It contains the silver dollar from George Shelby and a lock of Eva's hair. (Before she died, she had given one to each of her friends.) The ignorant and superstitious Legree is dismayed to see the lock of hair because he had received a lock of his mother's hair after she died. He had treated her shamefully, but with the lock had come a letter saying that on her deathbed she forgave her son and blessed him. He had burned that hair, and now drunk, he hurls Eva's into the flames. But that first time, as he watched, he had thought of everlasting fires. As time went by, drink, revel — nothing — would blot out the vision of his mother or the remembrance of the touch of her hair around his fingers. And now, in his stupor, he thinks it is his mother's hair that has come back. What if she herself should appear?

Legree is clearly alarmed, and to erase his woes and remorse and to prevent unpleasant visitations, he calls Sambo and Quimbo to join him in carousing. So soon there was heard "the sound of wild shriek-ing, whooping, hallowing, and singing, from the sitting-room, mingled with the barking of dogs, and other symptoms of general uproar." When Simon finally falls asleep, he has a nightmare about being pulled into a frightful abyss by dark hands; Cassy pushes him, and even his mother fails to help him.

The next morning Cassy tells him that is is poor business to beat Tom just when there is so much cotton to be picked; Cassy still has great influence over Legree. He is actually a little afraid of her because she is sometimes unbalanced (presumably due to the loss of her children and because of the nightmarish life she has led). So Simon goes to see Tom, bent on making the slave say he was wrong in refusing to flog Lucy. When Tom stands his ground, Legree threatens to burn him alive. Tom returns:

> Mas'r Legree, as ye bought me, I'll be a true and faithful servant to ye. I'll give ye all the work of my hands, all my time, all my strength; but my soul I won't give up to mortal man. I will hold on to the Lord, and put his com-

mands before all, — die or live; you may be sure on 't. Mas'r Legree, I an't a grain afeard to die. I'd as soon die as not. Ye may whip me, starve me, burn me, — it'll only send me sooner where I want to go.

Cassy intercedes as Simon fells Tom. For the time being, the owner decides to listen to Cassy.

The reader is now returned to the fortunes of George and Eliza. They are about to sail from Sandusky, Ohio, across Lake Erie to Canada. It has been learned from none other than slave catcher Tom Loker that Eliza's description is posted in Sandusky. To allay suspicion, Eliza is dressed as a young man and little Harry as a girl. Jim and his old mother have gone in a separate crossing.

What has changed Loker to the extent that he has actually helped the fugitives? Quakers took charge of him after he, having sustained injury, was abandoned by Marks and the others. Loker was so impressed with the treatment he received that on his recovery he decided to give up slave catching; he moved to a new settlement and engaged in trapping bears, wolves, and other animals.

Marks is still hoping to find the Harrises. He goes aboard their boat on the lookout for them, but the disguises work. He fails to recognize any of the family and goes ashore before sailing time. The ship moves closer and closer to Amherstburg, Canada, and Harriet writes of George:

> O, what an untold world there is in one human heart! Who thought, as George walked calmly up and down the deck of the steamer, with his shy companion at his side, of all that was burning in his bosom? The mighty good that seemed approaching seemed too good, too fair, even to be a reality; and he felt a jealous dread, every moment of the day, that something would rise to snatch it from him.
>
> But the boat swept on. Hours fleeted, and, at last, clear and full rose the blessed English shores; shores charmed by a mighty spell, — with one touch to dissolve every incantation of slavery, no matter in what language pronounced, or by what national power confirmed.

Back at Legree's plantation, as the days go by, Tom is subjected to the full vent of his owner's inhumanity. The poor slave is dejected almost to the point of losing his religious faith. And he is taunted:

> "You were a fool," said Legree; "for I meant to do well by you, when I bought you. You might have been better off than Sambo, or Quimbo either, and had easy times; and instead of getting cut up and thrashed,

every day or two, ye might have had liberty to lord it round, and cut up the other niggers; and ye might have had, now and then, a good warming of whiskey punch....

"You see the Lord an't going to help you; if he had been, he wouldn't have let *me* get you! This yer religion is all a mess of lying trumpery, Tom. I know all about it. Ye'd better hold to me. I'm somebody, and can do something!"

As the jeers continue, Tom has a vision of Christ, and he hears the words, "He that overcometh shall sit down with me on my throne, even as I also overcame, and am set down with my father on his throne." Tom's flagging faith is revived and "life's uttermost woes fell from his unharming." Legree sees that Tom is involved with the love of God, a force that he, Simon, cannot combat.

One night Cassy comes to Tom with a plan. She has drugged Legree and wants Tom to kill him with an axe:

"Not for ten thousand worlds, Misse!" said Tom, firmly, stopping and holding her back, as she was pressing forward.

"But think of all these poor creatures," said Cassy. "We might set them all free, and go somewhere in the swamps, and find an island, and live by ourselves; I've heard of its being done. Any life is better than this."

"No!" said Tom, firmly. "No! good never comes of wickedness. I'd sooner chop my right hand off!"

"Then *I* shall do it," said Cassy, turning.

"Oh, Misse Cassy!" said Tom, throwing himself before her, "for the dear Lord's sake that died for ye, don't sell your precious soul to the devil, that way! Nothing but evil will come of it. The Lord hasn't called us to wrath. We must suffer, and wait his time."

Tom finally dissuades the demented Cassy. He also suggests that she and Emmeline try to escape.

"I know no way but through the grave," said Cassy. "There's no beast or bird but can find a home somewhere; even the snakes and the alligators have their places to lie down and be quiet; but there's no place for us. Down in the darkest swamps their dogs will hunt us out, and find us. Everybody and everything is against us; even the very beasts side against us, — and where shall we go?"

Tom stood silent; at length he said, —

"Him that saved Daniel in the den of lions, — that saved the children in the fiery furnace, — Him that walked on the sea, and bade the winds be still, — He's alive yet; and I've faith to believe he can deliver you. Try it, and I'll pray, with all my might for you."

Cassy's spirit is lifted by Tom's words. She no longer rejects escape as hopeless and carefully plots flight for herself and the younger woman. Her plan depends largely on the air of superstition that pervades the run-down plantation. Years before, Simon had confined a slave woman for several weeks in the huge garret of his house. How he had tortured her there was not known, but it is indisputable that she died there. And after that, it was said that "oaths and cursings and the sound of violent blows used to ring through that old garret, and mingle with wailings and groans of despair." The musty garret has only one window and is the repository of furniture and large packing cases for furniture. But the Negroes are afraid to go near the garret, and the staircase and even the passageway to the staircase are avoided. Cassy now capitalizes on the old legend:

> In a knot-hole in the garret she had inserted the neck of an old bottle, in such a manner that when there was the least wind, most doleful and lugubrious wailing sounds proceeded from it, which, in a high wind, increased to a perfect shriek, such as to credulous and superstitious ears might easily seem to be that of horror and despair.

She tells Simon she has changed bedrooms to avoid weird noises coming from the garret. Then, once at midnight, when there is a high wind, Cassy opens the entry doors leading to the garret. Downstairs, Legree's candle is blown out, and he hears terrible noises. (Cassy had previously opened the garret window, knowing what would happen.) After that, the ignorant Simon had no desire to investigate the goings-on up there — exactly as Cassy had planned.

As part of their escape strategem, the two women go to the swamp that surrounds the plantation. They want to be seen there, because they know that whoever sights them will return to the house to raise an alarm. The plan works; while Legree is turning out the dogs and offering rewards for the capture of Cassy and Emmeline, the women return via a creek in back of the house. Cassy knows that the dogs will lose the scent in the water. The women are able to re-enter the empty house since everyone is out looking for them. Cassy uses the opportunity to remove a roll of bills from Legree's desk. (She will need money if her escape is to be successful.) The plan is to hide in the garret, where Cassy has stored all necessary provisions. She is confident that neither Simon nor any of the others will venture near the place they fear so much.

The next day Legree's search party, armed with guns, takes on people from neighboring plantations. They surround the swamp, but of course fail to find the fugitives. Simon's anger is centered on Tom, for he perceives that the slave knows something about Cassy's plans.

"Speak!" thundered Legree, striking him furiously. "Do you know anything?"

"I know, Mas'r; but I can't tell anything. *I can die!*"

Legree drew in a long breath; and, suppressing his rage, took Tom by the arm, and, approaching his face almost to his said in a terrible voice. "Hark 'e Tom! — ye think, 'cause I've let you off before, I don't mean what I say; but, this time, I've *made up my mind*, and counted the cost. You've always stood it out agin me: now, I'll *conquer ye or kill ye!* — one or t' other. I'll count every drop of blood there is in you, and take 'em, one by one, till ye give up!"

Tom looked up to his master, and answered, "Mas'r, if you was sick, or in trouble, or dying, and I could save ye, I'd *give* ye my heart's blood; and, if taking every drop of blood in this poor old body would save your precious soul, I'd give 'em freely, as the Lord gave his for me. Oh, Mas'r! don't bring this great sin on your soul! It will hurt you more than't will me! Do the worst you can, my troubles 'll be over soon; but, if ye don't repent, yours won't *never* end!"

Legree, Sambo, and Quimbo do their worst, but Tom stands firm. His last words to Simon are: "Ye poor miserable critter! There ain't no more ye can do! I forgive ye, with all my soul!" With that, he faints. Simon leaves the shed when he thinks Tom is dead. The other two repent; they wash Tom's wounds, place him on a rude, improvised bed, and even find him some brandy. Tom revives enough to tell them he forgives them. And Tom's abiding faith in Jesus makes converts of Sambo and Quimbo.

Young George Shelby, now master of Shelby, traces Tom to Legree's plantation, intending to buy him. But he arrives as Tom lies dying in the shed. There is a poignant reunion:

"You shan't die! you *mustn't* die, nor think of it. I've come to buy you, and take you home," said George, with impetuous vehemence.

"Oh, Mas'r George, ye're too late. The Lord's bought me, and is going to take me home, — and I long to go. Heaven is better than Kintuck."

"Oh, don't die! It'll kill me! — it'll break my heart to think what you've suffered, — and lying in this old shed, here! Poor, poor fellow!"

"Don't call me poor fellow!" said Tom, solemnly. "I *have* been poor fellow; but that's all past and gone, now. I'm right in the door, going into

> glory! Oh, Mas'r George! *Heaven has come!* I've got the victory! — the Lord
> Jesus as given it to me! Glory be to his name!"

When George makes disparaging remarks about Legree, Tom returns, "He ain't done me no real harm, — only opened the gates of the kingdom for me; that's all!" George sees that Tom gets a decent burial. To Legree he says:

> "I have not, as yet, said to you what I think of this most atrocious affair; — this is not the time and place. But, sir, this innocent blood shall have justice. I will proclaim this murder. I will go to the very first magistrate and expose you."
>   "Do!" said Legree, snapping his fingers, scornfully. "I'd like to see you doing it. Where you going to get witnesses? — how you going to prove it? — Come, now!"
>   George saw, at once, the force of this defiance. There was not a white person on the place; and, in all southern courts, the testimony of colored blood is nothing. He felt, at that moment, as if he could have rent the heavens with his heart's indignant cry for justice; but in vain.

Cassy and Emmeline eventually leave the garret disguised as ghosts. The older woman later dresses herself as a Creole Spanish lady, while the younger poses as her servant. They sail first on the Red River to the Mississippi and later transfer to a steamer going north. Cassy notes that George Shelby is also a passenger. She knows his relationship to Tom and feels that he can be trusted; so she takes him into her confidence.

The stateroom beside Cassy's is occupied by a Madame Emily de Throux and her 12-year-old daughter. Madame de Throux turns out to be the sister of George Harris, husband of Eliza. This mulatto woman has been freed by a man she was married to; he is now dead, and Madame de Throux, who has inherited an ample fortune from him, is on her way to Kentucky to look for George Harris. From George Shelby she learns that her brother has escaped to Canada. And there is another surprise; again from George, Cassy finds that her long-lost daughter Elise is none other than Eliza.

Emily and Cassy go to Amherstburg to search for the Harrises. The family is traced to Montreal, where George is working in a machinist's shop and doing well. Little Harry now has a sister, who appeals strongly to Cassy because the child is almost a replica of her Eliza at the same age. Commenting on the reunion, Harriet writes:

The note-book of a missionary, among the Canadian fugitives, contains truth stranger than fiction. How can it be otherwise, when a system prevails which whirls families and scatters their members, as the wind whirls and scatters the leaves of autumn? These shores of refuge, like the eternal shore, often unite again, in glad communion, hearts that for long years have mourned each other as lost. And affecting beyond expression is the earnestness with which every new arrival among them is met, if, perchance, it may bring tidings of mother, sister, child, or wife, still lost to view in the shadows of slavery.

Deeds of heroism are wrought here more than those of romance, when, defying torture, and braving death itself, the fugitive voluntarily threads his way back to the terrors and perils of that dark land, that he may bring out his sister, or mother, or wife.

One young man, of whom a missionary has told us, twice recaptured, and suffering shameful stripes for his heroism, had escaped again; and, in a letter which we heard read, tells his friends that he is going back a third time, that he may, at last, bring away his sister. My good sir, is this man a hero, or a criminal? Would not you do as much for your sister? And can you blame him?

Finding Eliza softens Cassy, and her dark moods disappear. Eventually the Harris family, Emily, Cassy, and Emmeline all move to France so that George can obtain a university education (financed by Emily). On the voyage, Emmeline meets a seafarer who later marries her. George's wish is to settle in Liberia. He writes to a friend:

It is with the oppressed, enslaved African race that I cast in my lot; and, if I wished anything, I would wish myself two shades darker, rather than lighter....

But, you will tell me, our race have equal rights to mingle in the American republic as the Irishman, the German, and the Swede. Granted, they have. We *ought* to be free to meet and mingle, — to rise by our individual worth, without any consideration of caste or color; and they who deny us this right are false to their own professed principles of human equality.

But, then, *I do not want it*; I want a country, a nation, of my own.

The remainder of the book gathers up the loose ends of the narrative. Miss Ophelia had returned to Vermont after the death of her cousin. There, under her tutelage, Topsy becomes a reliable young woman. In time she will go to Africa as a missionary. Through Emily, Cassy's son Harry is traced, and it is found that he has escaped to the North and will eventually join the family in Africa.

George Shelby's return is very painful for Chloe because she and the children were expecting Tom to be with him. (We recall that she had hired out to a confectioner in Louisville to earn money for Tom's freedom.) The best George could do was to describe to Chloe the circumstances of her husband's triumphant death and to relay his last messages of love for his family.

The final scene is the granting of freedom to all the slaves of the Shelby estate:

> "One thing more," said George, as he stopped the congratulations of the throng; "you all remember our good old Uncle Tom?"
>
> George here gave a short narration of the scene of his death and of his loving farewell to all on the place, and added, —
>
> "It was on his grave, my friends, that I resolved, before God, that I would never own another slave, while it was possible to free him; that no-body, through me, should ever run the risk of being parted from home and friends, and dying on a lonely plantation, as he died. So, when you re-joice in your freedom, think that you owe it to that good old soul, and pay it back in kindness to his wife and children. Think of your freedom every time you see UNCLE TOM'S CABIN; and let it be a memorial to put you all in mind to follow in his steps, and be as honest and faithful and Christian as he was."

The concluding remarks contain this observation:

> This is an age of the world when nations are trembling and convulsed. A mighty influence is abroad, surging and heaving the world, as with an earthquake. And is America safe? Every nation that carries in its bosom great and unredressed injustice has in it the elements of this last convulsion.

3

A Nation's Shame

Well may I say my life has been
One scene of sorrow and of pain.
From early days I griefs have known
And as I grew my griefs have grown.
— *Olaudah Equiano, 1789**

Over the centuries, slavery has existed in many forms and in many places. The modern world admires Greek culture, but it should be remembered that the glories of ancient Greece were in part supported by a slave system. In many cultures, captives taken in war, if they were spared, became slaves. Thus African chieftains often enslaved members of conquered tribes because they needed manpower. Under various governments, convicted criminals — who were public property — were sentenced to such places as the galleys and the mines. Sometimes criminals became indentured laborers whose sentences could be worked off. Until relatively modern times, a parent or guardian could sell a child, and a man could dispose of a wife or concubine in a like manner. Within the memory of many still living, Nazi Germany made expendable slave laborers of Jews, Slavs, and other conquered peoples, with no regard for their welfare.

Uncle Tom's Cabin deals with chattel slavery as it existed in the United States. This began in Africa before the American Revolution and concerns England in particular. (Other European powers, of course, engaged in the slave trade, but our interest here is in the British slave trade, which was responsible for the type of bondage existing in this country at its founding.)

*Equiano was stolen from an Ibo village when he was 11 and transported to the New World; he taught himself, purchased his freedom, and ultimately influenced the British antislavery movement.

Before the rise of the European slave trade, conquering Muslims sometimes shipped Africans to such places as Arabia and Persia. They were used mainly as servants, though some of the women were forced into harems and some of the men to various types of labor. Not all of these slaves were stolen; African chiefs who had been converted to Islam were known to sell their own people.

By as early as the end of the fourteenth century, the Spanish and Portugese were bringing Africans into Europe, using them chiefly as servants. But it was the New World that demanded an ever-increasing supply of manual labor to raise such crops as sugar, cotton, tobacco, indigo, and rice. In the course of history, whenever men have needed the service of other men, they have obtained it with the least possible cost to themselves. And so it was with the European colonists. Unsuccessful in forcing the Indians to work the land, they turned to the Negro. By the seventeenth and eighteenth centuries, the slave trade was carried on principally by the Dutch, French, and English. Trading posts were located along a portion of the western seaboard of Africa known as the Guinea Coast (see map), and from these points, millions of blacks were transported across the sea. Thus African slavery became bound up with the economic interests of some of the maritime nations of Europe.

Eventually England dominated the slave trade, which contributed enormously to her prosperity. A sailing vessel might leave one of the British ports bound for the Guinea coast with a cargo of liquor, firearms, cotton goods, and metal utensils. These would be traded, at a good profit, for items that included a cargo of humans. The second leg of the triangular voyage was known as the middle passage, and its destination was usually the West Indies. Provisions for this trip across the Atlantic were crucial, and the trading including such food as yams, fruit, kidney beans, coconuts, and corn. On arrival at a Caribbean port, the Negroes were exchanged, this time also at a profit, for agricultural products such as molasses, from which rum would be distilled. The last leg of the triangle was the return to England. Brady and Jones, in *The Fight Against Slavery*, point out the great economic importance of sugar production in the British economy; its value as a raw material can only be compared to that of oil in today's market. Eric Williams's *Capitalism and Slavery* shows the tremendous influence of the triangular trade on such home-country industries as sugar refining and on shipping, shipbuilding, and their ancillary trades. He attributes much of the

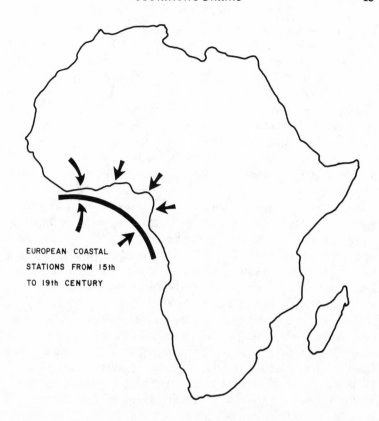

EUROPEAN COASTAL
STATIONS FROM 15th
TO 19th CENTURY

Africa and the slave trade. Inside arrows signify general inland raiding by Europeans. Courtesy Northern Michigan University, Cartographic Laboratory.

growth of the seaport towns of Bristol, Liverpool, and Glasgow to the same trade.

John Newton, who wrote the verses of several hymns, including the popular *Amazing Grace*,* had sailed on slavers, rising to the rank of captain. Since his writings provide valuable information about the triangular trade, we refer to them here.

A brigantine-type of ship, *The Duke of Argyll*, sailed from Liverpool on August 11, 1750, under Newton's command. He was then 25. Besides him, there were 39 aboard, including three mates, a

*Part of this is quoted in Uncle Tom's Cabin.

carpenter, and a doctor. The hold contained cheap cloth, metal bars, brandy, muskets, kettles, mirrors, and glass beads that were to purchase 200 slaves and a ballast of ivory and camwood. (The latter is the hard red wood of an African tree and was used as a dyewood.)

The trading lasted for three months, with Newton working through a European dealer. This was the usual procedure on the coast, but it should be noted that the inland trade was controlled by natives. For the most part, Africans sold into slavery were prisoners captured in tribal wars or kidnapped by slave raiders. Native kings and chiefs were not opposed to raiding nearby villages to obtain men and women who would bring them desired objects. Also, some tribes, as a form of punishment, condemned to bondage members who had committed adultery. And of course any unscrupulous individual might barter young and defenseless persons. In fact, one native did come aboard the *Argyll* with a young boy and girl for sale. The ship's doctor considered them worth two muskets, four kettles, and a bolt of cloth. He then attempted to have the man held as a slave also, but Newton refused to allow this.

The natives were brought to the trading post on foot, chained together in groups called coffles. Some may have come from great distances. (Obviously the numbers sought by the Europeans were scattered over a large area, and it is estimated that during the slave trade era, that area amounted to more than one-fifth of the entire African continent.) The blacks brought to the various trading centers or to the huge "castles" that came to be erected were, in general, members of agrarian tribes such as the Ibo, Ewe, and Biafra, and spoke a variety of languages or dialects. The diversity among those captured is aptly expressed by John Blassingame in *The Slave Community*: "Prince and peasant, merchant and agriculturist, warrior and priest, Africans were drawn into the vortex of the African slave trade...."

Following instructions from his English merchant, a Mr. Manesty, Newton bought captives that he considered robust and also those known to be artisans and craftsmen. The individuals selected were branded by a hot iron with the name of Manesty. (Those rejected were seldom set free; they were often murdered on the spot.)

Ship crews were in constant dread of being overpowered by their captives and took precautions to prevent this. Persons known to speak the same language were separated from each other, and periods of exercise on the deck were kept to a minimum. This meant that for most of the time the natives were in the airless, cramped hold that reeked. Aboard the *Argyll*, they were herded into a space measuring about 15 by 40 feet, and five feet high. The men were separated from the women by a rough bulkhead, and the compartments were divided horizontally into shelves for the Africans to lie on, one row above another. The Negroes were put in irons, two and two together, according to Newton, "the right hand and foot of one to the left of the other, but across — so that they cannot move either hand or foot, but with great caution and perfect consent." Shackled thus, the blacks were forced to lie in their own urine and feces during the middle passage; the average duration was around 60 days. The mortality (including suicides) for Africans on the middle passage averaged about 13 percent. Smallpox and dysentery were very common, and of course the frightful conditions below deck contributed to the spread of infectious disease. Also, with limited rations, malnutrition was widespread. When the captives were allowed on deck, they exercised to a whip.

One attempt to take over the vessel was promptly thwarted by Newton, with one of the leaders committing suicide and a young boy who was involved subjected to the thumbscrew. (Incidentally, had the Africans gained control of the *Argyll*, they would probably have perished unless they had some knowledge of sailing or navigation.)

The antislavery movement in England revealed some heinous incidents relative to the slave trade. One of these involved the *Zong*, which had begun the middle passage with 444 slaves. The voyage had taken longer than usual because of the captain's poor navigation. Sixty Africans had died, and food and water were running low. Intending to receive from the insurance underwriters full value for the 133 men and women who became sick, the captain threw them overboard.

It was always difficult to obtain crews for slavers, and Newton had some of the dregs of the waterfront. Even the doctor was drunk for most of the voyage (and died on the homeward trip). Crew losses were considerable, and the *Argyll* was no exception. When she returned to Liverpool on October 7, 1751, only 16 of the original crew remained, with two extra hands taken, in exchange, from a warship.

By the time Newton landed in St. John's in Antigua, 28 of the Africans had died during the voyage. (Seventeen had succumbed even before the ship set sail.) After disposing of his human cargo, Newton turned his energy to the return trip. This time it was sugar, tobacco, mahogany, rum, and spices, all of which brought great gain.

As an aside, we mention here that John Newton gave up the sea and became an Anglican minister. A product of a harsh age and one who had endured injustice and flogging in the British Navy, he was for some time unmoved by the violence and atrocities of the slave trade — "During the time I was engaged in the slave trade I never had the least scruple as to its lawfulness." But in time he realized its injustice and became committed to its abolition. His pamphlet, *Thoughts upon the African Slave Trade*, recounts his experience as a common seaman on a slaver, as a trader on the Guinea Coast, as mate and master on a slave ship, on the plantation, and with the Liverpool merchants. His account was fair and credible and became an important document in the British fight against slavery.

Authorities differ in their estimations of how many natives were forced from Africa by the slave trade. It is certainly several million, with a large preponderance of males. Some historians believe that deaths before ships left the coast, deaths during the middle passage, and deaths due to the breaking-in period in the New World were so numerous that each slave working in America cost the life of another.

The slave trade continued until 1807, a period of almost four centuries. It destroyed nations such as Benin, Songhay, and Mali along with their languages, art, and religion. John Hope Franklin notes in *From Slavery to Freedom* that civilization had reached a high point on the African West Coast at the time when European traders were demanding the healthiest, the largest, the youngest, the ablest, and the most culturally advanced. Thus the expatriation of millions of Africa's best people was a far-reaching and drastic revolution that tragically affected the subsequent development of that continent.

A Dutch frigate transported the first Africans to British America; however, these 20 blacks who arrived in Jamestown, Virginia, in 1619 were indentured servants. Such persons (more often English and white) were given free passage to America and in return agreed to work without pay for a specified period. Once the period of servitude was ended, they were usually assigned some land to cultivate, and above all, they were free. This type of arrangement was not unusual; in fact, by 1683 one-sixth of the population of the 13 colonies was indentured. It is noteworthy that the census of 1623 and 1624 listed the blacks in Jamestown as *servants*, not slaves.

However, as pointed out by Avery Craven in *The Coming of the Civil War*, the laws regarding this temporary bondage were a groundwork for attitudes about slavery. For example, a 1619 Virginia law upheld the employer's right to administer corporal punishment, and later the servant's right to marry was restricted.

It was soon evident that indentured servitude would not supply adequate labor to clear the forests and grow the tobacco crops envisaged by the Virginia planters. These men knew that the sugar plantations in the Caribbean were maintained by slave labor; so they gradually turned toward this source. In South Carolina and Georgia, rice cultivation required slave labor; by 1771 as much as 65 million pounds per year were being exported, with profits exceeding those for tobacco. In 1740, South Carolina planters began to grow indigo for the British wool industry, and this crop also drew slave labor. But for a short period, free labor, slavery, and indentured servitude existed together in colonial America. This is of interest because later, free labor in the American West resisted competition with slave labor. And gradually it was assumed that all blacks were slaves.

After 1660 the colonies began to pass laws that legalized Negro slavery. Dwight Dumond's *Antislavery* notes that the basic slave code of the English colonies was written in Barbados in 1688; during the eighteenth century this harsh code was adopted, with minor modifications in some cases, by South Carolina, Georgia, and Florida. Slaves were much less numerous in New England, and the codes there were, in general, less severe.

The importation of blacks to the colonies increased until the mid-1700s, when the cultivation of tobacco slowed down. But the invention of the cotton gin in 1791 ended any hope that slavery would disappear for economic reasons. By separating the seeds from fibers, the cotton gin made profitable the production of vast amounts of cotton. (Gin is short for engine.) To plant and pick it, an ever-increasing supply of slave labor was needed.

The Declaration of Independence proclaimed that liberty is an inalienable right of all men. Apparently this liberty did not apply to the Negro. Thomas Jefferson, though a slaveowner himself, saw the danger to the Union inherent in the existence of slavery. He wrote to John Adams that the surfacing of the issue over the admission of Missouri "like a firebell in the night, awakened and filled me with terror." Though the Declaration failed to mention abolition, a suppressed section did criticize George III as follows:

> He has waged cruel war against human nature itself, violating its most
> sacred rights of life and liberty in the persons of a distant people who never
> offended him, captivating and carrying them into slavery in another hemi-
> sphere, or to incur miserable death in their transportation thither. This
> piratical warfare, the approbrium of *infidel* powers, is the warfare of the
> Christian king of Great Britain.

David Davis in *The Problem of Slavery in Western Culture* em-
phasizes that England never required her colonists to buy slaves, and
that the original and essential grievance of the colonists involved was
that they could not buy enough slaves at a reasonable price. Obviously the continuation of slavery was of great importance to the
southern colonies, but the northern colonies were using slaves too,
although in much smaller numbers. The North had also encouraged
slavery in other ways. To illustrate, rum distilleries flourished in New
England, requiring ships to carry sugar from the Caribbean and ships
to export the finished product. The trade with the West Indies thus
employed, directly or indirectly, thousands — seamen to sail the ships
and artisans to supply them. So perhaps it is not surprising that the
Continental Congress rejected the section quoted; it might have
proved a source of embarrassment to a nation that failed to halt this
"cruel war."

The Constitutional Convention of 1787 also had to face the
slavery issue. George Mason, a Virginia delegate and slaveholder,
said at his state's ratifying convention: "As much as I value a union of
all the states, I would not admit the Southern States into the Union
unless they agree to the discontinuance of this disgraceful trade...."
Mason, incidentally, did not sign the Constitution.

Other delegates held similar views; Gouverneur Morris of
Pennsylvania called the slave trade "a definance of the most sacred
laws of humanity." Luther Martin of Maryland left the convention in
disgust because he saw the influence of the southern slaveowners and
the northern shippers combining to extend the existence of the trade.
James Madison, a slaveholder opposed to slavery, did not wish to
admit the existence of forced bondage by using the word "slave" in
the Constitution.

By compromise, the convention agreed that the slave trade
could continue for another 20 years. With regard to direct Federal
taxation and fixing representation, it was decided that 100 slaves
would count as 60 white persons. Note how the word slave is
avoided:

Representatives and direct Taxes shall be apportioned among the several States which may be included within the Union, according to their respective numbers, which shall be determined by adding to the whole Number of free Persons, including those bound to Service for a Term of Years, and excluding Indians not taxed, three fifths of all other Persons.

Such equivocation would cause endless debate over whether or not the Constitution sanctioned slavery, debate that ended only with the enactment of the Thirteenth Amendment.

During the Revolutionary War, Lord Dunmore, the British governor of Virginia, offered freedom to Negroes who would fight for the Crown. About 800 enlisted. As the war progressed, many slaves escaped to the British lines or just ran away. Dunmore's offer alarmed the Americans, and eventually all states except Georgia and South Carolina were offering manumission in exchange for a set period of military service. It is estimated that about 5,000 blacks fought for the United States in the War of Independence.

When Harriet Beecher (not yet Mrs. Stowe) moved to Cincinnati in 1832, Ohio was a free state. (The Ordinance of 1781 had prohibited slavery in the then Northwest Territory, which encompassed the region west of Pennsylvania, north of the Ohio River, east of the Mississippi and south of the Great Lakes.) Thus, when slavery existed in Ohio, it was illegal. However, especially after 1850, fugitive slaves found in the state could be reclaimed by their owners. (This is why Harriet's character Eliza was anxious to get her son to Canada.) But slavery was legal in Delaware, the District of Columbia, Maryland, Virginia, North Carolina, South Carolina, Georgia, Alabama, Mississippi, Louisiana, Arkansas, Missouri, Kentucky, and Tennessee; Florida and Texas were also admitted as slave states.

By 1830 the number of slaves in this country exceeded two million and was increasing at a rate of about 30 percent each decade, attributable almost entirely to reproduction. Domestic slave trading became profitable after the foreign trade was closed, beginning January 1, 1808. Despite the latter event, around 5,000 Africans were still being smuggled into the United States every year.

The slave population was concentrated in areas where staple crops could be raised in large quantities. (To the alarm of the white population, there were counties in Alabama and Mississippi where blacks outnumbered whites.) Of these staple crops, cotton was the

most important, and by the 1840s it was the major agricultural product of Mississippi, Alabama, South Carolina, Georgia, and Florida.

Some slaves worked on farms and some were hired out by owners who pocketed their wages, but the majority of them lived on plantations that produced cotton. These unfortunates labored without recompense from sun up to sun down, except on Sunday. Women were not spared, even while nursing their babies. Incidentally, they were often required to nurse the children of the master also. Slaves lived in crowded, one-room huts, usually without beds and sometimes even without enough covering to keep warm. They were supplied a bare minimum of food and clothing, just enough to survive, for their labor was valuable. And they were encouraged to multiply, for surplus offspring could be sold for profit. The plantation was virtually their prison, since freedom of movement was rarely granted; they were denied education and sometimes the Bible; legally binding marriages were prohibited, and children born to slaves did not belong to them, but became the property of the master. In short, slaves were chattel to be sold at will, a situation that often caused family members to be separated forever. Overseers ruled with whips and other instruments of torture.

To the modern reader, corporal punishment seems barbaric. But, as noted by Albert Bushnell Hart in *Slavery and Abolition*, flogging was legal toward apprentices, and in some communities, toward wives. It was a common punishment throughout the South for the less-serious crimes committed by white people. (The Navy abolished flogging only in 1850.)

A southern local historian has warned that generalization is often the pitfall that traps the scholar trying to analyze the many facets of slavery. Naturally there were some good and humane slave owners, and conditions varied from plantation to plantation, farm to farm, and so on. *Plantation, Town and County*, edited by Miller and Genovese, points this out. House slaves, exemplified by Harriet's characters Eliza and Chloe, usually fared better than field hands. Some slaves were taught to read and write, as was the character Cassy; most learned about God. With regard to this, Southerners sometimes justified slavery by saying that they had rescued heathen

Opposite: Picking cotton in Mississippi. Post-Civil War painting. Courtesy Library of Congress.

and given them the benefits of Christianity. Christianity did not grant freedom, but it is recognized that religion played a major role in the lives of many Negroes. By the nineteenth century, the branding of colonial days was rarely done. But the inherent evil of the system is clear from a sentence in the Louisiana Code: THE SLAVE IS ENTIRELY SUBJECT TO THE WILL OF HIS MASTER. In short, in the so-called land of the free, slavery had become, in the words of Dumond, "the complete subjection by force of one person to the will of another, recognized and sustained by state law." There was no security for the slave. Lydia Maria Child, an abolitionist writer, expressed this well in 1836:

> And let it never be forgotten that the negro's fate depends entirely on the character of his master; and it is a mere matter of chance whether he falls into merciful or unmerciful hands; his happiness, nay, his very life depends on chance.

Thus there was no redress when an unscrupulous master or overseer made unreasonable demands on the enslaved man, woman, or child. Sometimes a good master died or went bankrupt, with the result that his slaves were put up for sale. (Harriet's Uncle Tom was sold for both reasons.) Sometimes a kindly master, frequently absent from his plantation, was not aware of the atrocities of his overseer.

To see that the slave codes were obeyed, patrols of white men apprehended and often harassed any slave found away from the plantation of his owner. Failure to produce the required pass could mean jail or return to the master. Clearly the slave faced, at best, a grim future subject to uncertainty, and there was little to enforce his self-esteem. In addition to all this, as the state laws became more repressive in the South, legal freedom, known as manumission, became more difficult to obtain.

In 1839 a book entitled *American Slavery As It Is* was published anonymously. The facts it contained were obtained from newspapers of the slave states and from statements by responsible persons who had resided in the slave states, some of whom were former slave-holders. The author was Theodore Dwight Weld, a prominent abolitionist about whom there will be more in the next chapter. The book is obviously biased in favor of the abolitionist viewpoint, but it provides much valuable information about conditions in the South during the first half of the nineteenth century. This is a perceptive comment by a lawyer from Ohio who spent a year in Florida:

> The Negro has no other inducement to work but the lash; and as man never acts without motive, the lash must be used so long as all other motives are withheld. Hence corporal punishment is a necessary part of slavery.

A Connecticut minister who had lived in slave states for 14 years described the slave's turmoil at day's end about the required quota of cotton. This scene is reminiscent of the fictional one in *Uncle Tom* where Tom gives a woman some cotton from his basket.

> You will see them, with their baskets of cotton, slowly wending their way to the cotton house, where each one's basket is weighed. They have no means of knowing accurately, in the course of the day, how they make progress; so that they are in suspense, until their basket is weighed. Here comes the mother with her children; she does not know whether herself, or children, or all of them, must take the lash; they cannot weigh the cotton themselves — the whole must be trusted to the overseer. While the weighing goes on, all is still. So many pounds short, cries the overseer, and takes up his whip....

(In a general way, the overseer's salary was proportional to the size of the cotton crop.)

A Quaker carpenter who had lived in South Carolina described beatings he witnessed:

> Having occasion to pass a plantation very early one foggy morning in a boat, we heard the sound of the whip, before we could see, but as we drew up in front of the plantation, we could see the negroes at work in the field. The overseer was going from one to the other causing them to lay down their hoe, strip off their garment, hold up their hands and receive their number of lashes. Thus he went from one to the other until we were out of sight.

A teacher from Ohio who had worked in Louisiana described the plight of a slave who attempted to escape:

> One of [Nowland's] slaves ran away, and came to the Homo Chitto river, where he found no means of crossing. Here he fell in with a white man who knew his master, being on a journey from that vicinity. He induced the slave to return to Baton Rouge, under the promise of giving him a pass, by which he might escape, but in reality, to betray him to his master. This he did, instead of fulfilling his promise. Nowland said he took the slave and inflicted five hundred lashes upon him, cutting his back all to pieces, and

then threw on hot embers. The slave was on the plantation at the time, and told me the same story.

Disregard for separating family members is shown by this advertisement that appeared in the *New Orleans Bulletin*:

> NEGROES FOR SALE — A negro woman 24 years of age, and has two children, one eight and the other three years. Said negroes will be sold separately or together *as desired*. The woman is a good seamstress. She will be sold for cash, or *exchanged* for groceries.

This ad reminds us that Harriet's character Emmeline was parted from her mother at a slave auction.

Southerners denied the existence of widespread miscegenation. However, miscegenation did exist; according to the 1850 census, approximately eight percent of the slave population were mulattoes. The status of the mulatto child followed that of the mother, which meant that a master sometimes sold his own son or daughter into the bondage of another white man. An Illinois man who had lived for 32 years in North Carolina wrote this: "Amalgamation was common. There was scarce a family of slaves that had females of mature age where there were not some mulatto children."

James L. Smith, born a slave, was presumably about the same age as Harriet. He managed to escape and around 1880 wrote his autobiography. His memory of earlier events and scenes may not be accurate, and his account may have been altered to suit the viewpoint of the editor. However, the following appears reasonable:

> Our dress was made of tow cloth; for the children, nothing was furnished them but a shirt; for the older ones, a pair of pantaloons or a gown, in addition, according to the sex. Besides these, in the winter season an overcoat, or a round jacket; a wool hat once in two or three years for the men, and a pair of coarse brogan shoes once a year. We dwelt in log cabins, and on the bare ground. Wooden floors were an unknown luxury to the slave. There were neither furniture nor bedsteads of any description; our beds were collections of straw and old rags, thrown down in the corners; some were boxed in with boards, while others were old ticks filled with straw. All ideas of decency and refinement were, of course, out of the question.
>
> Our mode of living in Virginia was not unlike all other slave states. At night, each slept rolled up in a coarse blanket; one partition, which was an old quilt or blanket, or something else that answered the purpose, was extended across the hut; wood partitions were unknown to the doomed

slave. A water pail, a boiling pot, and a few gourds made up the furniture. When the corn had been ground in a hand-mill, and then boiled, the pot was swung from the fire and the children squatted around it, with oyster shells for spoons. Sweet potatoes, oysters and crabs varied the diet. Early in the morning the mothers went off to the fields in companies, while some women too old to do anything but wield a stick were left in charge of the strangely silent and quiet babies. The field hands having no time to prepare any thing for their morning meals, took up hastily a piece of hoe-cake and bacon, or any thing that was near at hand, and then, with rakes or hoes in the hand, hurried off to the fields at early dawn, for the loud horn called them to their labors. Heavy were their hearts as they daily traversed the long cotton rows. The overseer's whip took no note of aching hearts.

The allowance for the slave men for the week was a peck-and-a-half of corn meal, and two pounds of bacon. The women's allowance was a peck of meal, and from one pound-and-a-half to two pounds of bacon; and so much for each child, varying from one-half to a peck a week, and of bacon, from one-half to a pound a week. In order to make our allowance hold out, we went crabbing or fishing. In the winter season we used to go hunting nights, catching oysters, coons and possums.

Frederick Douglass, the most eminent black American of the nineteenth century, described years later the scene of a slave appraisal following the death of his Maryland owner:

What an assemblage! Men and women, young and old, married and single; moral and intellectual beings, in open contempt of their humanity, leveled at a blow with horses, sheep, horned cattle, and swine! Horses and men — cattle and women — pigs and children — all holding the same rank in the scale of social existence; and all subjected to the same narrow inspection, to ascertain their value in gold and silver — the only standard of worth applied by slaveholders to slaves! How vividly, at that moment, did the brutalizing power of slavery flash before me! Personality swallowed up in the sordid idea of property! Manhood lost in chattelhood!

... Our destiny was now to be *fixed for life*, and we had no more voice in the decision of the question, than the oxen and cows that stood chewing at the haymow. One word from the appraisers, against all preferences or prayers, was enough to sunder all the ties of friendship and affection, and even to separate husbands and wives, parents and children. We were all appalled before that power, which, to human seeming, could bless or blast us in a moment.

Linda Brent (pseudonym) was a Negro who escaped from slavery at age 27 and became active in the antislavery movement. She also belonged to Harriet's era. Her story was edited by Lydia Maria Child and published in 1861. This was Linda's observation on sexual assault on the bondswoman by her owner:

Even the little child, who is accustomed to wait on her mistress and her children, will learn, before she is twelve years old, why it is that her mistress hates such and such a one among the slaves. Perhaps the child's own mother is among those hated ones. She listens to violent outbursts of jealous passion, and cannot help understanding what is the cause. She will become prematurely knowing in evil things. Soon she will learn to tremble when she hears her master's footfall. She will be compelled to realize that she is no longer a child. If God has bestowed beauty upon her, it will prove her greatest curse. That which commands admiration in the white woman only hastens the degradation of the female slave....

John Calhoun, the renowned statesman from South Carolina, referred to slavery in the South as a "peculiar domestic institution." As the framers of the Constitution had avoided the word "slave," Southerners by the 1830s were using the euphemism "peculiar institution" to refer to their cruel and repressive type of slavery. Historians have noted that the South maintained a "conspiracy of silence" about it, as far as was possible.

By 1830 there were about 319,000 free Negroes in the United States, most of whom lived in urban areas. Some had been born in free states, some even in slave states where the child of a free mother and a slave was free. Others had purchased their freedom or were manumitted by an owner's will or through a deed of manumission. The southern states were, in general, opposed to manumission, fearing that the presence of free blacks might encourage slaves to run away or to revolt.

Some of this fear has been attributed to Denmark Vesey. Vesey had purchased his freedom in 1800 and had managed to earn his living as a carpenter. He was familiar with the Haitian slave revolt, and over a period of years organized for July, 1822, a massive uprising of city and plantation slaves who lived in the city of Charleston, South Carolina. Pike heads, bayonets, and daggers were collected, because if slaves were to be freed, killing of whites and destruction of property would take place. The plan was aborted because a black warned white authorities in time. Vesey and many Negroes were hanged or deported. A few whites were fined and imprisoned for their part in the insurrection.

Seven years after Vesey's ill-fated venture, both South and

Opposite: Slave auction at Richmond, Virginia. Courtesy Library of Congress.

North were shaken by a pamphlet written by another free black, David Walker. Born in North Carolina, Walker had settled in Boston where he sold second-hand clothing on the waterfront. The following is an excerpt from his 1829 appeal, addressed "particularly to the Colored citizens":

> Kill or be killed. Had you rather not be killed than to be a slave to a tyrant who takes the life of your wife and children? Look upon your wife and children and mother and answer God Almighty, and believe this that it is no more harm to kill a man who is trying to kill you than to take a drink of water when you are thirsty.

The free Negro received harsh treatment not only in the South but in the North also. Many states did not permit residence after manumission; many also restricted or prohibited the immigration of free blacks. Some southern states imposed registration, a white guardian, and the like. Most states required "free papers" to be available at all times; this was necessary because those in authority had the attitude, expressed in 1821 by the New Jersey Supreme Court, that black men were to be considered slaves unless proven otherwise. Kidnapping a freedman was not uncommon because a white man's word was much more likely to be taken than a black man's. Economic advancement was very difficult; white artisans, for example, resented employment of free Negroes and certain occupations were closed to the latter. The right to vote was frequently denied. Although required to support public education in some localities, the free black might find that his children were barred from school.

During the eighteenth century, various persons with various motives had advanced the idea of transporting free sons of Africa to what was later termed "the land of their fathers." There was precedent from England.

In 1772 the so-called Somerset decision abolished slavery in the British Isles (but not in the colonies). After the American Revolution, British antislavery leaders chose what is now the republic of Sierra Leone to resettle Negroes who had been brought to England as slaves, but who now were free. The early groups to be transported included blacks from the colonies and some white prostitutes from London. Eventually the British government took over Sierra Leone, ruling it until it gained its independence in 1967. In 1815 Paul Cuffe, an enterprising free black from the United States, settled 38 free American Negroes in Sierra Leone at his own expense. This did much to spark interest in an American colonization movement.

The next year The American Society for the Colonization of the Free People of Colour of the United States (American Colonization Society) was formed, with its first president Bushrod Washington, Supreme Court Justice and nephew of George Washington. Henry Clay, then Speaker of the House, was a vice-president. Attorney Francis Scott Key, author of the poem *Star-Spangled Banner*, among others, lent assistance. Following the suggestion of British abolitionists, the location of the new colony was down the West Africa coast from Sierra Leone and today is known as Liberia. The capital was named Monrovia in honor of the man who was president when Liberia was established. Added support for the movement came when the Anti-Slave Trade Act of 1819 provided for a naval patrol off the African coast and the resettlement in Africa of Negroes captured while being illegally imported to the United States. Congress appropriated $100,000 for Liberia which remained under the control of the American Colonization Society until its independence in 1847.

The Liberian colonists suffered great hardship. The first area selected was an island that proved unsuitable because of problems with the drinking water and in clearing the tropical vegetation. In 1820 the site was moved to the mainland. There the settlers were beset by malaria and other diseases, unfriendly tribes, unfamiliar pests, and a very hot climate with 200 inches of rain per year. Many died, but gradually the colony prospered.

From the standpoint of the United States, African colonization was not successful. Between 1820 and 1860 the society spent $1,806,000 to carry there only about 11,000 Negroes. According to Hart, it would have cost $700 million to remove the four million United States slaves whose labor alone was worth the $700 million.

Very significant was the fact that, despite the inhospitable climate in this country, most free Negroes wished to remain here, the land of their birth. In 1817, for instance, 3,000 met in Philadelphia to register their objections to colonization, branding the operation an "outrage, having no other object in view than the benefit of the slave-holding interests of the country."

From the beginning, the motives of the colonization were suspect. Some of them are stated here in a letter written in 1817 by Robert Goodloe Harper, a Baltimore lawyer, to the society:

In reflecting on the utility of a plan for colonizing the free people of color, with whom our country abounds, it is natural that we should be first struck by its tendency to confer a benefit on ourselves, by ridding us of a population for the most part idle and useless, and too often vicious and mischievious.

The slave, seeing his free companion live in idleness, or subsist, however scantily or precariously, by occasional and desultory employment, is apt to grow discontented with his own condition, and to regard as tyranny and injustice the authority that compels him to labor.

Here [the free blacks] are condemned to a state of hopeless inferiority and consequent degradation. As they cannot emerge from this state, they lose by degrees the hope and at last the desire of emerging.... The few honorable exceptions serve merely to show of what the race is capable in a proper situation. Transplanted to a colony composed of themselves alone, they would enjoy real equality: in other words, real freedom. They would become proprietors of land, master mechanics, shipowners, navigators, and by degrees, schoolmasters, justices of the peace, militia officers, ministers of religion, judges, and legislators....

To such arguments the militant David Walker replied:

Will any of use leave our homes and go to Africa? I hope not. Let no man of us budge one step, and let slave-holders come to beat us from our country. America is more our country, than it is the whites — we have enriched it with our *blood and tears*. The greatest riches in all America have arisen from our *blood and tears*: — and will they drive us from our property and homes, which we have earned with our *blood*?

In 1834 Judge William Jay published his views on the colonization society. He saw three different aims, each from a different class of people:

First, such as desire sincerely to afford the free blacks an asylum from the oppression they suffer here, and by this means to extend the blessings of Christianity and civilization to Africa, and who at the same time flatter themselves that colonization will have a solitary influence in accelerating the abolition of slavery. Secondly, such as expect to enhance the value and security of slave property, by removing the free blacks; and thirdly, such as seek relief from a bad population without the trouble or expense of improving it.

After the so-called debates held on slavery at Lane Theological Seminary in 1832 (see Chapter 4), colonization was rejected in favor of the abolitionists' concept of immediate emancipation, sometimes referred to as immediatism. Harriet's critics have pointed out that, writing in 1851, she insulted blacks by sending the Harris family to Africa. Modern historians contend that support of colonization implied belief in the racial inequality of the black. It is undeniable that many Caucasians of that time considered the Negro race inferior; in fact, in 1858, Abraham Lincoln stated that the Negro "is not my equal in many respects — certainly not in color, perhaps not in moral or intellectual endowment." As late as his presidency he was considering colonization. While trying to enlist the support of certain eminent free Negroes, he said to them, "Your race suffer greatly, many of them, by living among us, while ours suffer from your presence. In a word, we suffer on each side. If this is admitted, it affords a reason why we should be separated." Today the idea of racial inequality in the Negro is unacceptable to any thinking person. But it should be remembered that antebellum Americans could not be familiar with the accomplishments of a Booker T. Washington, a Ralph Bunche, or a Marian Anderson.

By 1840 the North was becoming increasingly industrialized. The successful manufacture of cotton cloth, spun by power looms, spurred the growth of New England cities such as Lowell, Massachusetts. Linen and wool manufacture also became important where water power was combined with an opportunity to ship finished products. The iron industry grew as anthracite and bituminous coal replaced charcoal and coke for smelting. The growth of the textile and iron industries alone created a demand for machinery. The region also had mines, forges, mills, ships, and a burgeoning population due to the influx of European immigrants, particularly from Ireland. To protect infant home industries from foreign competition, Congress, under Clay's leadership, imposed tariffs.

In contrast to the North, the South remained rural and agrarian, with its wealth in land and slaves. It exported cotton to New England, but mainly to England. In conjunction with the latter, it imported from Europe factory-made products for which the average duty amounted to 40 percent; so obviously the protectionism favored by Northerners was far from popular with Southerners.

Although agriculture was the major occupation, the application of scientific methods was minimal. Edmund Ruffin, a Virginian, advocated the use of lime and manure to improve impoverished land such as resulted from continuous tobacco cultivation, but his advice was for the most part ignored. Crop rotation was not understood; cotton and corn were usually rotated, a practice that was unproductive. Ordinarily, when soil became exhausted, it was abandoned and new land broken. This sometimes necessitated a move to the southwest to obtain the desired virgin soil.

Plantations produced most of the staple crops of the South. Rice and cotton have been mentioned. By 1850, Kentucky, Tennessee, and Mississippi were raising large amounts of tobacco. Sugar cane was grown in Louisiana, and hemp in Kentucky. (It will be recalled that the character George Harris in *Uncle Tom* was hired out by his master to work in a bagging factory in Kentucky.) Plantations were more or less isolated, and each had at least 30 slaves, and some many more. The envied and powerful planter class consisted of only about 25,000 men. Most slave owners possessed five slaves or less and worked with them in the fields; but apparently many of these owners dreamed of becoming planters. Three-fourths of the South's population were small farmers with no slaves; the poor whites owned neither slaves nor land. Frederick Douglass commented on the slave's attitude toward this white caste system: "To be a slave was thought to be bad enough, but to be a poor man's slave, was deemed a disgrace, indeed."

Corn was a very important crop to the Southerner, accounting for more acreage and having greater value than cotton, rice, and tobacco combined. It was used to make corn bread, corn pone, hominy grits, and whiskey, and was also fed to animals. The dried husks could be split into shreds and used in mattresses rather than straw. Other crops included wheat, oats, rye, flax, and both white and sweet potatoes.

Unlike the owner, the slave seldom had much incentive to work. In such a situation, conflict was inevitable, and many considered the system inefficient. Booker T. Washington, who was born into slavery in 1856, makes an interesting observation on plantation life:

> The whole machinery of slavery was so constructed as to cause labour, as a rule, to be looked upon as a badge of degradation, of inferiority. Hence labour was something that both races on the slave plantation sought to escape. The slave system on our place, in a large measure, took the spirit of self-reliance and self-help out of the white people. My old master had many boys and girls, but not one, so far as I know, ever mastered a single trade or special line of productive industry. The girls were not taught to cook, sew or to take care of the house. All of this was left to the slaves. The slaves, of course, had little personal interest in the life of the plantation, and their ignorance prevented them from learning how to do things in the

most improved and thorough manner. As a result of the system, fences were out of repair, gates were hanging half off the hinges, doors creaked, window-panes were out, plastering had fallen but was not replaced, weeds grew in the yard. As a rule, there was food for whites and blacks, but inside the house, and on the dining-room table, there was wanting that delicacy and refinement of touch and finish which can make a home the most convenient, comfortable, and attractive place in the world. Withal there was a waste of food and other materials which was sad. When freedom came, the slaves were almost as well fitted to begin life anew as the master, except in the matter of book-learning and ownership of property. The slave owner and his sons had mastered no special industry. They unconsciously had imbibed the feeling that manual labor was not the proper thing for them. On the other hand, the slaves, in many cases, had mastered some handicraft, and none were ashamed, and few unwilling, to labour.

In 1831 a Virginia slave named Nat Turner led a revolt that caused the death of more than 60 whites. Turner and about 20 other blacks were hanged, and repercussions were severe in that throughout the South slave codes became more and more restrictive. At about the same time, slave owners began to defend their "peculiar institution" with more vehemence, although many of the arguments had been offered before. Their defense was partly in response to rising criticism from the abolitionists.

Calhoun said that censure had caused the South

> to look into the nature and character of this great institution, and to correct many false impressions that even we had entertained in relation to it. Many in the South once believed that it was a moral and political evil; that folly and delusion are gone; we see it now in its true light, and regard it as the most safe and stable basis for free institutions in the world.

Here are the sentiments of a group of intellectuals. Chancellor William Harper of the College of South Carolina declared slavery "a principal cause of civilization," noting that under it Greece and Rome had prospered. John Hammond, who would become governor of South Carolina, contended that:

> In all social systems there must be a class to do the menial duties, to perform the drudgery of life.... Its requisites are vigor, docility, fidelity. Such a class you must have or you would not have that other class which leads progress, civilization, and refinement.

George Holmes, who later became a professor, maintained that whereas exploitation of labor in the North represented materialism, slavery

> protects those that require protection — the young, the aged and the infirm. It resists the tendency to convert all life and all social action into a mechanism for the mere augmentation of gain, and directs the minds and hearts of men to other more elevated objects.

In an age when almost all authority for action was referred to the Bible, it was to be expected that proslavery people would quote Scripture to support their stand. One favorite was Genesis 9, verses 18–27, where Noah, waking from a drunken sleep, said to his son Ham, who was father of Canaan, "Cursed be Canaan, a servant of servants shall he be unto his brethren." He also said, "Blessed be the Lord God of Shem; and Canaan shall be his servant." There seemed to be no difficulty with interpreting this to mean that Ham's descendants would be slaves and black, while those of his brother Shem (and of Japeth) would be white! A little easier to understand is the claim that Leviticus 25, verses 44–46 clearly permitted the Jews to buy bondsmen and bondswomen. And in a society that saw the will of God in all events, St. Paul's exhortation (1 Corinthians, 8, 20) to "let every man abide in the same calling wherein he was called," was interpreted as favoring the continuance of slavery. (Harriet has Wilson quote this to Harris.)

Underlying the foregoing sentiments is again the assumption of the racial inferiority of the Negro. Some Southerners showed a real interest in ethnology. One of these was Josiah Nott, a Mobile physician who had black patients. In 1844 he gave two lectures on his theory that the Negro and the white man were of different species, the second being superior to the first. Darwin's *Origin of the Species* was not published until 15 years later, and such a belief indicates how little was known about biology and anthropology.

Another proslavery viewpoint is expressed in *A Girl's Life in Virginia*, written by Letitia Burwell in 1895. The real-life slaves she describes lived rather like the mythical ones belonging to St. Clare in *Uncle Tom*:

> The master's residence — as the negroes called it, "the great house" — occupied a central position and was handsome and attractive, the overseer's being a plainer house about a mile from this.

Plantation scene. Wood engraving, 184?. Courtesy Library of Congress.

Each cabin had as much pine furniture as the occupants desired, pin and oak being abundant, and carpenters always at work for the comfort of the plantation.

Bread, meat, milk, vegetables, fruit, and fuel were as plentiful as water in the springs near the cabin doors.

Among the negroes — one hundred — on our plantation, many had been taught different trades; and there were blacksmiths, carpenters, masons, millers, shoemakers, weavers, spinners, all working for themselves. No article of their handicraft ever being sold from the place, their industry resulted in nothing beyond feeding and clothing themselves.

The mistress here, however, was no Marie St. Clare. According to Letitia Burwell, her mother's

cares and responsibilities were great, with one hundred people continually upon her mind, who were constantly appealing to her in every strait, real or imaginary. But it had pleased God to place her here, and nobly did she perform the duties of her station. She often told us of her distress on realizing for the first time the responsibilities devolving upon the mistress of a large plantation, and the nights of sorrow and tears these thoughts had given her.

Another excerpt from the same book reflects several attitudes common to the day. It also reminds us again that Uncle Tom was first sold unwillingly to Mr. Shelby, but of necessity, to pay off a debt:

> There was a class of men in our State who made a business of buying negroes to sell again farther south. These we never met, and held in horror. But even they, when we reflect, could not have treated them with inhumanity; for what man would pay a thousand dollars for a piece of property, and fail to take the best possible care of it? The "traders" usually bought their negroes when an estate became involved, for the owners could not be induced to part with their negroes until the last extremity—when everything else had been seized by their creditors. Houses, lands,—everything went first before giving up the negroes; the owner preferring to impoverish himself in the effort to keep and provide for these,—which was unwise financially, and would not have been thought of by a mercenary people.
>
> But it was hard to part with one's "own people," and to see them scattered. Still our debts had to be paid,—often security debts after the death of the owner, when all had to be sold. And who of us but can remember the tears of anguish caused by this, and scenes of sorrow to which we can never revert without the keenest grief? Yet, like all events in this checkered human life, even these sometimes turned out best for the negroes, when by this means they exchanged unpleasant for agreeable homes. Still it appeared to me a great evil, and often did I pray that God would make us a way of escape from it. But His ways are past finding out, and why He had been pleased to order it thus we shall never know.

In general then, southern life was based on agriculture, and the South wished to continue this way of life, which needed slavery to carry it on. As the North became more industrialized, Southerners feared loss of economic power and became more determined than ever to retain slavery.

4

A House Divided

I am confident not many years will roll by before the horrible traffic in
human beings will be destroyed in this land of Gospel privileges.
— Diary of Angelina Grimké, 1835

Many active in the nineteenth-century antislavery movement
criticized the Christian church for failing to take a stand against an
institution that so flagrantly violated the tenets of the New Testament. Harriet was one of these. Nevertheless, the religious fervor of a
handful of men and women gave great impetus to the antislavery
movement. Harriet herself was also one of these.

The Quakers were the first sect to make an official condemnation of slavery. As early as 1676 in a general letter to Friends in slave-
holding colonies, another Quaker named William Edmundson
recommended emancipation. At the time Edmundson was living in
Rhode Island, a Quaker stronghold, but previously he had been a
missionary to slaves in Barbados, where his ministry had incurred
the hostility of the planters. Twelve years later, some Quakers of
Germantown, which is now part of Philadelphia, wrote a *Remon-
strance Against Slavery and the Slave Trade*. Then in 1693 George
Keith, once an associate of George Fox, had confronted others of his
faith with his *Exhortation and Caution to Friends Concerning Buying
and Keeping of Negroes*. Many Quakers were prosperous slaveholders — William Penn bought and sold slaves — and Keith was
urging them to free their slaves. He was not popular, nor were other
Quakers who individually advocated the same action. By 1737
Benjamin Lay's diatribes on slavery and slaveholders were no better
received. But the Quakers professed to believe that all men and all
women were equal before God, a belief that was in conflict with men

holding their brother men in bondage. Also, a member of the Society
of Friends based his actions on the "inner light" that was in reality
his own conscience. Although the objections cited had little immediate effect, the Quaker conscience was gradually aroused. Action
finally came through the influence of two Quakers who were in
prominent positions during the three decades preceding the War of
Independence.

The first is Anthony Benezet. This man was a French Huguenot
born in 1713. He lived in Philadelphia and was a schoolteacher. But
his fame rests on the antislavery tracts he wrote for distribution in
both America and England. These influenced, among others,
Thomas Clarkson, who became one of the prime movers in Britain's
fight against slavery; Granville Sharp, another English reformer who
won a case establishing that a slave was free on reaching England;
and John Wesley, the founder of Methodism. About the slave trade
Benezet wrote that "nothing can be more inconsistent with the
Doctrines and Practice of our meek Lord and Master, nor stained
with a Deeper Dye of Injustice, Cruelty and Oppression."

The second Friend of note was John Woolman, a tailor from
New Jersey. A gentle and almost saintly man, he traveled exten-
sively, often on foot, to spread his antislavery message. Disdaining
anything that in any way involved slave labor, he refused to eat
sugar or to wear dyed apparel. He managed to persuade many
Quakers to free their slaves and, on the Rhode Island coast, brought
his doctrine to shipowners involved in slavetrading. (He also urged a
better land policy for Indians and tried to stop the sale of rum to
them.)

Whereas Benezet was considered an antislavery publicist,
Woolman moved people by his sincerity and personal example. Here
are two excerpts from Woolman's *Some Considerations of the
Keeping of Negroes. Part the Second,* 1762:

> Men, taking on the government of others, may intend to govern reason-
> ably, and make their subjects more happy than they would be otherwise;
> but, as absolute command belongs only to him who is perfect, where frail
> men, in their wills, assume such command, it hath a direct tendency to
> vitiate their minds and make them more unfit for government.
>
> A covetous mind, which seeks opportunity to exalt itself, is a great
> enemy to true harmony in a country; envy and grudging usually ac-
> company this disposition, and it tends to stir up its likeness in others. And
> where this disposition ariseth so high, as to embolden us to look upon

honest industrious men as our own property during life, and to keep them
to hard labor, to support us in those customs which have not their foundation in right reason; or to use any means of oppression; a haughty spirit is
cherished on one side, and the desire for revenge frequently on the other,
till the inhabitants of the land are ripe for great commotion and trouble;
and thus luxury and oppression have the seeds of war and desolation in
them.

The theme of the first paragraph — that power corrupts — would
be reiterated time and time again by the abolitionists, and the theme
of the second paragraph — God's vengeance — would also appear
frequently and finally find sublime expression in Lincoln's Second
Inaugural Address.

At last, in 1774, the Philadelphia Yearly Meeting of the Society
of Friends adopted rules forbidding Quakers to buy or sell slaves and
requiring Quakers to prepare those they held in bondage for
freedom. This caused considerable sacrifice, because many Friends
had investments in activities dependent on slavery. A year later in
Philadelphia, Quakers founded the Society for the Relief of Free
Negroes Unlawfully Held in Bondage.

Once the Friends took a stand, antislavery activity gained
strength; also during the eighteenth century, the rational thinkers of
the Enlightenment were critical of slavery. By 1785 the New York
City Manumission Society had been organized, and four years later
Benjamin Franklin founded the Pennsylvania Abolition Society. But,
as mentioned previously, the invention of the cotton gin in 1791 was
a serious deterrent to progress toward emancipation.

By the nineteenth century even serfdom was disappearing in
Europe, and the spirit of freedom was moving westward. Haiti
became independent in 1804 after a violent slave revolt in 1796. By
1848 the French government had abolished slavery in the islands. The
revolutions that freed large areas of Latin America from Spain led to
emancipations in the new republics. The Spanish government,
however, continued to sanction slavery in its remaining possessions,
and abolition did not come until 1888. The British fight for emancipation affected mainly slavery in her colonies; in the United States, of
course, the conflict involved slavery that was still legal in a large area
of home territory. But in the two countries the antislavery approaches were somewhat similar and at times intertwined.

In England the legal struggle began with the work of Granville
Sharp, an ordnance clerk of unusual ability and humanitarianism.

He sought to determine that slavery was illegal on British soil, and after making a thorough study of the law decided to force such a ruling from Baron Mansfield, Lord Chief Justice at that time. He was successful in 1772. The case involved James Somerset, a slave brought to England from Virginia. Rather than return to the plantation, he had run away. But his master had found him and was intending to send the black to Jamaica for sale. Sharp intervened, and Mansfield had to make a decision. The jurist knew that there were then in England about 20,000 slaves worth around 700 pounds sterling to the planters who owned them. Mansfield hesitated for months; as Abraham Lincoln would be later, he was confronted by a dilemma, one horn representing property rights, the other civic rights. He finally ruled that the state of slavery

> is so odious that nothing can be suffered to support it but positive law. Whatever inconveniences, therefore, may follow from this decision, I cannot say this case is allowed or approved by the law of England. And therefore the black must be discharged.

Sharp carried on a trans-Atlantic correspondence with Benezet that led to communication between English and American antislavery advocates. Later he worked for the establishment of a colony for free blacks in Sierra Leone. The Somerset decision initiated a political struggle that would last for 51 years.

A pivotal figure in this struggle was Thomas Clarkson, who in 1787 began his visits to British ports to collect facts about the slave trade. Despite threats against him, he continued to gather much important evidence—evidence that necessitated his riding great distances on horseback. He applied skill, energy, and perseverance to his task. The facts he found "filled me both with melancholy and horror," and they were used effectively by Wilburforce in Parliament. Clarkson, who was greatly influenced by the writings of Benezet, became an authority on the slave trade; besides crusading for its abolition, he worked to improve the frightful lot of the British sailor.

William Wilburforce was a personal friend of Prime Minister William Pitt the Younger. At Pitt's request, Wilburforce undertook the leadership in Parliament to abolish the slave trade. When at last in 1789 the proposal came to vote in the House of Commons, it was defeated overwhelmingly. This was not surprising; the abolitionists were taking on enormous vested commercial interests as well as what Pitt termed "all the bigotry and ignorance with which our country is so generously endowed."

This was the first of several defeats, but Wilburforce was not to be deterred. Considered sanctimonious by many, he was a religious man with a cause, but no political ambitions. In his favor, antislavery sentiment was increasing. The Quakers were exemplary in their efforts; abolition societies were formed and antislavery tracts and pamphlets distributed; antislavery petitions were flooding Parliament; even prominent figures such as religious reformer John Wesley, economist Adam Smith, and poet William Cowper had written against slavery. Indeed, in 1786 Josiah Wedgwood of pottery fame had struck an antislavery cameo that was becoming more and more familiar in England. During the Napoleonic Wars, when Pitt deserted the abolition cause and turned his attention to the protection of British rights, the movement seemed doomed to failure. But victory came in 1807 when both houses voted to prohibit Britain's participation in the slave trade.

Wilburforce and his followers believed that stopping the supply of African slaves to America would ultimately end slavery in the New World (the United States Congress also abolished the slave trade in 1807), but this view was unrealistic. Violations of the law were common; the regulation did not apply to Brazil and Cuba, for example, and there was still the problem of those already in bondage.

Economic forces were now aiding abolition as the price of East India sugar rivaled that grown in the Caribbean. It was expected that a declining market for sugar from the West Indies would reduce opposition to emancipation. Humanitarians were becoming increasingly impatient with the concept of gradual emancipation. In 1824 the Scottish Quaker, Elizabeth Heyrich, wrote *Immediate, Not Gradual Abolition*, a publication that influenced many, including William Lloyd Garrison, who would become a great American abolitionist.

Wilburforce, after some years of relative inactivity in the cause, did begin to work for emancipation in the early 1820s. When he retired from the Commons in 1825, the able Thomas Fowell Buxon succeeded him in Parliament as the leader for abolition. At long last, in 1833, a law was passed to free all slaves in the British colonies after a five- to seven-year period of apprenticeship, with compensation to their masters. Wilburforce had died two days before the vote, but he

was aware of the great debate in progress and of the strong possi-
bility that his long struggle would mean a lasting victory.

While the passage of the Bill for the Abolition of Slavery
prompted many Englishmen to extol their country's virtue, other
Britons must have agreed with Charles Darwin who wrote: "It makes
one's blood boil ... that we Englishmen and our American descendants with their boastful cry of liberty, have been and are so
guilty."

During the nineteenth century, various types of American
reform movements came into being, their existence due largely to
humanitarian and religious impulses. In the mid-1820s in upstate
New York, a great revival was spearheaded by Charles Grandison
Finney, lawyer turned evangelist. Finney taught that on conversion
the moral obligation of a Christian was to attack sin; sin concerned
both personal indulgence and social evil. Finney's importance to the
abolitionist movement lies in the fact that many of his followers
would use the techniques of the great revival to fight slavery, which
these same followers regarded as sin. Authorities have pointed out,
for example, that the "immediate repentance" of revivalism became
the "immediate emancipation" of abolitionism, and that the itinerant
evangelist became the antislavery agent. Finney converted thousands, among them Theodore Dwight Weld, whom we have
mentioned and shall meet again soon. And he helped to lay the
foundation for the reform spirit that swept the country.

It was around this time that William Lloyd Garrison, then 22,
met Benjamin Lundy, an antislavery Quaker publisher. A New
Englander of rather obscure origin, Garrison had been a printer and
was then the editor of a Boston temperance paper. Lundy was a long-
time supporter of gradual emancipation and believed in colonization;
he had even visited Haiti, as well as Mexico and Canada, in search of
a suitable location for free blacks. It is likely that Lundy's ideas
influenced Garrison, because when Garrison became the editor of the
Bennington, Vermont, *Journal of the Times*, it was on the condition
that he could discuss abolition, temperance, peace, and moral reform
in addition to politics. The next year Edward Beecher, Harriet's
oldest brother and then pastor of Boston's Park Street Church,
invited Garrison to his pulpit to give a Fourth of July address. Instead
of extolling the nation, the guest speaker criticized it for participating
in the crime of slavery. He reminded his audience:

A very large proportion of our colored population were born upon our soil, and therefore entitled to the privileges of American citizens. This is their country by birth, not adoption. Their children possess the same inherent and inalienable rights as ours....

He also indicated the duty of the North:

The free states—by which I mean the nonslaveholding states—are constitutionally involved in the guilt of slavery, by adhering to a national compact that sanctions it; they have the right to remonstrate against its continuance, and it is their duty to assist in its overthrow.

But he warned that if a person thinks that

slavery can be abolished without a struggle with the worst passions of human nature, ... he cherishes a delusion.... Sirs, the prejudices of the North are stronger than those of the South; they bristle, like so many bayonets around the slaves; they forge and rivet the chains of the nation. Conquer them, and the victory is won.

He also made the assumption

that education and freedom will elevate our colored population to a rank with the white—making them useful, intelligent and peaceable citizens.

John Scott in his *Hard Trials on My Way* points out that Harriet, then just 18, heard that address.

Soon afterward Garrison joined Lundy in Baltimore where he wrote articles for Lundy's *Genius of Universal Emancipation*. He remained there less than a year and was forced to spend some of that time in jail because of conviction in a libel suit concerning the domestic slave trade. During this period he became adamantly opposed to colonization, which he had supported and which Lundy continued to support. In 1832 Garrison's *Thoughts on African Colonization* was published and served to turn antislavery thinking against colonization. We should note here that all abolitionists, here and in England, were obviously against slavery; but in this country the term abolition came to be associated with the immediate emancipation supported by Garrison and Weld.

Abolitionists leaned heavily on speeches, newspapers, pamphlets, and petitions to alter public opinion. In Boston, on New Year's Day, 1831, the first issue of Garrison's own antislavery paper, the *Liberator*, came out, the type set by the publisher himself. He announced:

> I *will be* as harsh as truth, and as uncompromising as justice. On this subject [slavery] I do not wish to think, or speak, or write with moderation. No! No! Tell a man whose house is on fire to give a moderate alarm; tell him to moderately rescue his wife from the hands of a ravisher; tell the mother to gradually extricate her babe from the fire into which it has fallen; —but urge me not to use moderation in a cause like the present. I am in earnest—I will not equivocate—I will not excuse—I will not retreat a single inch—AND I WILL BE HEARD. The apathy of the people is enough to make every statue leap from its pedestal, and to hasten the resurrection of the dead.

The issue contained material urging abolition, and there was criticism of allowing slaveholding in the District of Columbia. *The Liberator* ran until 1865; most of the subscribers were free blacks. Although the circulation was never more than 2,500, various other newspapers exchanged with it, and editors, both northern and southern, often quoted from it. Garrison proved himself a master in the editorial combats popular with journalists of the day. And his writing naturally riled the South; to illustrate, a Georgia slaveholder wrote to the editor of the *Liberator*: "I now ask you, will you desist? or shall I be compelled to ride more than 1,000 miles to put a period to the rascality of so base, infamous, abominable, traitorous, lawless, unprincipled, impudent, degraded, cowardly a dog as you are?"

The reader may recall that Nat Turner's insurrection took place only a few months after the debut of the *Liberator*. The fear engendered by the rebellion may have been responsible for the increased southern opposition to Garrison's writings. In fact, Georgia in 1831 appropriated $5,000 "to be paid to any person or persons who shall arrest, bring to trial and prosecute to conviction, under the laws of this state, the editor or publisher of a certain paper called the *Liberator*." Very soon it became clear that Garrison's hope to persuade slaveholders to emancipate their slaves was doomed to failure. Even north of the Mason-Dixon line* his views were not popular; for example, in 1835 he was attacked in Boston by an anti-abolitionist mob.

Originally this referred to the boundary between Pennsylvania and Maryland. Later the term was used with regard to free or slave states.

William Lloyd Garrison, 1805–79. Courtesy Boston Public Library, Print Department.

Garrison, always noted for his piety, believed steadfastly in the teaching of the New Testament. Quoting St. Paul that in Jesus Christ, all are one; there is neither Jew nor Gentile, bond nor free, male nor female, he stood for racial equality and for equality of the sexes. He was also a pacifist. His religious fervor did not deter him from expressing contempt for clergymen who upheld slavery. (But he shocked Boston with his view that observance of the Sabbath was "an outworn and foolish superstition.")

As time passed, Garrison became more radical. As early as 1832, he was suggesting that the North should withdraw peacefully from the Union because the Constitution legalized slavery. Ten years later the masthead of the *Liberator* had a new slogan: "A Repeal of the Union between Northern Liberty and Southern Slavery is Essential to the Abolition of the One and the Preservation of the Other." On July 4, 1854, he publicly burned a copy of the Constitution, to which he had referred as "a covenant with death and agreement with Hell." Since Garrison refused to recognize the Constitution in any way, he did not vote for any political candidate who would swear to defend it, and he would have liked to prevent other abolitionists from doing so. His thinking along these lines was influenced by John Humphrey Noyes's so-called perfectionist doctrine.

Many who favored emancipation came to distrust Garrison's approach. They believed that the issue of slavery was so important that the fight against it should not be diverted by attention to other issues of great interest to Garrison—for instance, women's rights and temperance. As we shall see, the women's movement gained strength in antislavery effort; Garrison, unlike many of the abolitionists, believed in the equality of the sexes. There were other reasons for discontent with the man that was regarded as a fiery editor: his *Liberator* was notorious for its belligerent and extravagant language; he carried on unceasing war with the clergy; he was often difficult to deal with. But the greatest reason for dissatisfaction was his unyielding anticonstitutionalism. Many abolitionists began to realize that the moral crusade advocated by Garrison was not effective enough. Political action was necessary, and Garrison was hostile to this. (Nevertheless, despite this and his pacifism, he supported Lincoln— with reservations, it is true—and the Civil War.) It cannot be denied that Garrison, whatever his weaknesses, attracted to his cause many capable and talented men, a number of whom later broke with him. He always had support from the New England Antislavery Society, which he founded and which had many women members. He was also highly regarded by the British public, whose aid he enlisted on behalf of abolition and, later, of Lincoln.

Historians today disagree about the extent of Garrison's influence. One who denigrated him was historian Gilbert Hobbs Barnes, who in 1933 referred to Garrison as a "figurehead of fanaticism." But few can disagree with the comment of Russel Nye, an authority on Garrison's era:

> Garrison, more than any other person, shattered the "conspiracy of silence." One might decry his invective, censure his methods, or deny his

appeal to disorder; one could never shut out his clamor. To disagree with Garrison men had to face up to the problem, rethink their beliefs, examine their own consciences. When men did this, slavery was doomed. Garrison contributed relatively little to the philosophy of abolitionism. He had only one single thought — that "slavery was a crime, a damning crime" — but he made other men think, though he sometimes muddled their thinking. Economic and political events that Garrison neither knew nor cared about made slavery a national issue and precipitated the war. But it had its moral causes too, which Garrison's career aptly symbolized to the victorious North.

Harriet, too, used the written word to make the North face up to the problem of slavery. It is interesting that Nye notes, with regard to Garrison and Harriet, that neither seemed quite able to understand what the other was trying to do.

Another abolitionist of note was Theodore Dwight Weld. Although Weld and Garrison were roughly the same age, their modes of action were very different. The son of Congregational minister, Weld at an early age showed an aptitude for lecturing, a gift very much in demand in his day. When he was 22 he entered Hamilton College in New York state. Soon afterward he was converted by the revivalist Charles Grandison Finney, whom we mentioned earlier. Weld became devoted to Finney, traveling with him, learning from him, and even helping him with conversions.

Another Finney follower was Charles Stuart, a retired British military man who lived in Utica. Stuart and Weld, despite a considerable age difference, struck up a firm friendship. After Stuart returned to Britain in 1829 to work for British abolition, he wrote Weld beseeching him to enlist in the American antislavery movement. Stuart also sent him some antislavery literature used in England. Weld by now had decided to enter the ministry, and again at Stuart's suggestion, he left Hamilton to enroll at Oneida Institute where he appears to have functioned as a part-time student. Oneida required piety, service to mankind, and manual labor, all of which were to Weld's liking. A week's board could be paid for with 20 hours of work; Stuart also contributed. Weld, older than most of the students, was in charge of the milking crew. Also, because of his oratorical talent, he was often sent on fund-raising tours, and he frequently lectured on temperance. Apparently he had little time for study because his parents, as well as Stuart, urged him to be less active in outside activities.

During this period Weld met another Finney convert, Lewis Tappan, who was the father of two Oneida students. Lewis and his brother Arthur were prominent philanthropists, contributing much of the fortune they had earned in dry goods to reforms of the day. Although narrow in their religious thinking, they were enthusiastic and generous when some unpopular causes were involved. The brothers were impressed with Weld's leadership and persuasive abilities and invited him to New York City, having in mind a pastorate for him. Weld refused this, but in 1831 did become the general agent for their Society for Promoting Labor in Literary Institutions. He was now 28 and still had not completed his studies; however, Weld had a burning desire to reform mankind, and an association with the Tappans would certainly mean opportunities in this line. He was instructed to visit schools and colleges to obtain information on how to combine study with manual labor. He quickly changed from investigating to proselytizing for the cause of manual labor. He concentrated on what is now the Midwest because, like Lyman Beecher, he considered this the most important section of the expanding nation. He also toured the South, learning much about slavery. He traveled by stagecoach and riverboat but also covered hundreds of miles on horseback and sometimes even went on foot. Accommodations were often poor or nonexistent. Twice he had close calls in stagecoaches, once when fording a swollen current and once when a drunken driver ran the stage off the road and down an eight-foot bank. In Alabama Weld spent a month at the home of a slave-holding Presbyterian minister. Here he met James G. Birney, whom he would convert to abolitionism and who would become the Liberty Party's twice-nominated candidate for the presidency on a platform for emancipation. But at the time, both Weld and Birney still favored colonization.

In 1832 when Weld visited Western Reserve College in Hudson, Ohio, he found some faculty members who were already embracing the doctrine of immediate emancipation: President Storrs, who had been receiving the *Liberator* for several months, and two professors, Elizur Wright, a mathematician, and Beriah Green, a minister, both of whom would become important figures in the abolition crusade. They won Weld to their thinking, and later a letter from Wright contained the suggestion that Weld devote his considerable talent to pressing for immediate emancipation.

This was exactly what Weld did, but his course was rather

unusual. His study of educational institutions suited to the fostering of manual labor completed, he enrolled as a theology student at the newly established Lane Seminary in Cincinnati. (There is evidence that Lane's financial agent considered Weld more an advisor than a student, since Weld seems to have had influence on how the Tappan money was spent. At any rate, it is clear that the young zealot was both forceful and resourceful in dealing with both the Tappans and the Lane authorities.) Arthur Tappan had promised money if Lyman Beecher would accept the presidency. Weld and the Tappans viewed Lane as an ideal institution to promote both manual labor and anti-slavery sentiment. The first theology class consisted of 40 members; 30 of these were more than 26 years old. A number were followers of Finney and 24 had come from Oneida Institute, where Weld had been. Most were unusually mature and appear to have been devoted to Weld. Beecher recognized Weld's influence among the students, but the older man apparently underestimated the importance of the slavery issue.

In February, 1834, Lane's student body, prompted by Weld, debated the question "Ought the people of the slave-holding states to abolish slavery immediately?" The meetings were evangelical in nature and lasted for two and one half hours a night over 18 successive nights. Students gave first-hand accounts of slavery in various states, and one account was furnished by a free black who had been a slave. Half of the debates concerned the position of colonizationists. The vote was in favor of immediate abolition. Weld worked assiduously behind the scenes, while on the platform his persuasive oratory did much to undermine colonization. He believed that "faith without *works* is dead," and the students formed an organization to elevate and instruct the free blacks of Cincinnati, of whom there were more than 1,000. In other parts of the North, attempts to educate the Negro had stirred fierce resistance, and it was no different in the Ohio city. Besides trying to educate the blacks, the students now openly walked the streets with Negroes of both sexes. Weld actually boarded with some of them. He, like Garrison, was a true believer in racial equality. Many abolitionists, then and later, were not so advanced in their thinking, though they did wish to see the black man educated. Some Cincinnati inhabitants became alarmed at this new acceptance of what they considered an inferior breed.

We should note that Harriet, still Miss Beecher, was in Cincinnati at this time and doubtless knew of these events. Her future

husband, Calvin Stowe, was a professor at Lane and one of her father's right-hand men. Dr. Beecher believed that information, argument, and moral persuasion would in time influence the slaveholding states to free their slaves. He also realized that the presence of free black agents would present problems to the South — and also to the North if they chose to go there — so he grasped at colonization as a workable solution. He, along with many others of his day, feared that abolitionist recklessness would produce violence and even the ultimate dissolution of the Union. In fact, when Garrison, years before, had tried to enlist the preacher's help, he had been refused. On the other hand, when the question of admission of Negroes to Lane came up, Beecher's position was:

> Our only qualifications for admission to the seminary are qualifications intellectual, moral, and religious, without reference to color, which I have no reason to think would have any influence here, certainly never with my consent.

And, as mentioned, there was in the student body a black who had been able to purchase his freedom.

Beecher tried to discourage the social intercourse that he knew was so odious to the local populace (even some advanced thinkers of the day condemned intermarriage), but to no avail. However, he was confident that the unruly followers of Weld would tire of their crusade and return to their studies.

He was mistaken. Many of them remained in the city during the summer that followed. One of Cincinnati's frequent cholera epidemics broke out, causing fear and despair. Tempers were short anyway, but matters came to a head with a newspaper editorial that censured the white divinity students for inviting black girls to picnic with them on the seminary premises. Beecher was in the East on a fund-raising tour when a few harried board members announced that the student organization could no longer exist and even forbade discussion of the slavery issue. They informed the press of their action, which gained Lane a reputation for having proslavery leanings. President Beecher returned to find the students in revolt against the trustees. He and Stowe tried to patch things up, but it was no use.

Opposite: The Tappan brothers (left: Arthur, 1786–1865; right: Lewis, 1788–1873). Courtesy Schomburg Center, New York Public Library.

Forty of them, including Weld, withdrew from the institute. Weld's complaint was that free speech had been denied. Most of his band moved on to Oberlin College, which became associated with the abolitionist movement. Lane never recovered from the bad publicity and loss of students. To compound the trouble, the Tappans transferred their financial support to Oberlin.

Now abolitionism had footholds in New England, the middle Atlantic states, and the Midwest. Noting the success of the British antislavery movement and persuaded by Weld, the Tappan brothers and other abolitionists founded the American Antislavery Society in Philadelphia in 1833. A few Negroes and some Quaker women were present. Among the latter was Lucretia Mott, who later would become a leader in the feminist movement. For the next seven years the American Antislavery Society was destined to be a strong force in the fight for emancipation. Its Declaration of Sentiments was drawn up by Garrison. The goal was, of course, the abolition of slavery in the United States. The new organization would send out agents to educate about immediate emancipation, to distribute tracts, and to organize local societies (by this time, however, the South would not tolerate such agents). The society's official publication was known as *The Emancipator*, and Elizur Wright was brought from Ohio to New York to manage affairs. Membership was open to individuals who subscribed to the society's principles and paid dues, and thus the American Antislavery Society was more than a federation of state or local abolitionist societies.

After his withdrawal from Lane, Weld, in October, 1834, became a traveling agent for the American Antislavery Society at a salary of $8 per week plus expenses. An ex-Lane student named Augustus Wattles remained in Cincinnati to organize work with the Negroes. Arthur Tappan came to the rescue as usual by providing some eastern women teachers, while some local ladies aided the work by volunteering time.

Weld's mission was to convert Ohio to abolitionism. We have noted his gift for persuasive oratory; he viewed slavery as a sin, and he aimed to make others see it in the same light. Night after night he lectured "with the utmost precision and fluency...," his voice "wonderful in its compass and power." Later the *Pittsburgh Times* reported that his "inexhaustible fund of anecdotes and general information—with the power of being intensely pathetic, enables him to give the greatest imaginable interest to the subject." If denied the

Theodore Dwight Weld, 1803–1895. Courtesy Library of Congress.

use of a church, he might use a barn. He was unmoved by hostile and angry mobs. There was now increasing resistance from Northerners who had ties with the South and from Northerners who looked down on and feared the Negro. Finney himself, for example, feared a civil war, and the Columbus *Ohio State Journal* characterized abolitionist doctrine as "tending directly to a civil war and a dissolution of the Union by breaking up the original pact." When additional agents were needed, Weld found them at Oberlin. He taught them his techniques and used them often during vacation periods. He was very successful, especially with rural audiences. How successful is apparent from the report of the annual meeting of the American

Antislavery Society held on May, 1836. Ohio had 133 abolition
societies compared to New York's 103 and Massachusetts's 87. Henry
B. Stanton, who had worked with Weld at Lane and would marry
feminist Elizabeth Cady, was also a success in Rhode Island.

Now the society undertook to train and commission 70 agents to
finish the conversion of the North, again recruiting many of the Lane
students who had gone to Oberlin. Weld organized the training,
calling in to assist such people as Stanton and Garrison. The 70
included James Birney, who by now had forsaken colonization and
was editing an abolitionist paper, and a woman from South
Carolina, Angelina Grimké, who was accompanied by her sister
Sarah. Their story will appear in the next chapter. The 70 became
depleted in number for various reasons—a severe financial panic in
1837 for one—but the smaller band that was sent out did much to
make the North sensitive to the great issue dividing the nation.

Abolitionist editors now faced mob violence in the North. In
1835 it was vented on Garrison in Boston; in 1836 on Birney in
Cincinnati; and in 1837 on Elijah Lovejoy in Alton, Illinois. (The last act
had a profound effect on Edward Beecher, who witnessed Lovejoy's
defense and death and wrote a moving account of the event.)

During 1834–35 the American Antislavery Society concentrated
on the distribution of literature that would "awake the conscience of
the nation to the evils of slavery." Mailing lists were drawn from
newspapers, public records, membership rosters of organizations,
and the like. The South was determined that such reading matter
would never reach slaves (of whom, ironically, only a handful could
read). In 1835 a citizens committee in Charleston burst into a post
office, removed American Antislavery Society mailings, and burned
them. Various southern legislatures then began to appeal to their
northern counterparts. Virginia's request is typical:

> Resolved, that the State of Virginia has a right to claim prompt and effici-
> ent legislation by her co-states to restrain as far as may be, and to punish,
> those of their citizens, who, in defiance of the obligations of social duty and
> those of the Constitution, assail her safety and tranquility, by forming as-
> sociations for the abolition of slavery, or printing, publishing, or circulat-
> ing through the mail or otherwise, seditious and incendiary publications,
> designed, calculated, or having a tendency to operate on her population,
> that this right, founded as it is on the principles of international law, is
> peculiarly fortified by a just consideration of the intimate and sacred re-
> lations that exist between the States of this Union.

Postmaster General Amos Dresser of Kentucky was of little help. He admitted that he had no authority to prohibit abolitionist literature from the mail, but added:

> We owe an obligation to the laws, but a higher one to the communities in which we live, and if the former be perverted to destroy the latter, it is patriotism to disregard them....
>
> There is reason to doubt whether these abolitionists have a right to make use of the mails of the United States to convey their publications into the states where their circulation is forbidden by law, and it is by no means certain that the mail carriers and Postmasters are secure from the penalties of the law if they knowingly carry, distribute, or hand them out.

One of the most prominent abolitionist orators was Wendell Phillips, who supported Garrison until 1865 when they broke over support for Lincoln's policies. Here is an excerpt from an 1853 speech by Phillips on the philosophy of the abolitionist movement:

> What is the denunciation with which we are charged? It is endeavoring, in our faltering human speech, to declare the enormity of the sin of making merchandise of men, of separating husband and wife, taking the infant from its mother, and selling the daughter to prostitution, of a professedly Christian nation denying, by statute, the Bible to every sixth man and woman of its population, and making it illegal for "two or three" to meet together, except a white man be present!
>
> The South is one great brothel, where half a million of women are flogged to prostitution or, worse still, are degraded to believe it honorable. The public squares of half of our great cities echo to the wail of families torn asunder at the auction block; no one of our fair rivers that has not closed over the Negro seeking in death a refuge from a life too wretched to bear; thousands of fugitives skulk along our highways, afraid to tell their names, and trembling at the sight of a human being; free men are kidnapped in our streets, to be plunged into that hell of slavery....

The most famous of the abolitionist publications was Weld's *American Slavery As It Is*, mentioned in the preceding chapter. One hundred thousand copies of this exposé, in which the South is made to condemn itself, were sold in the first year of publication. Historian Dwight Dummond has termed this work "in all probability the most crushing indictment of any institution ever written." According to her own statement, Harriet was familiar with it; how much it influenced *Uncle Tom's Cabin* is unclear. Weld's biographer, Benjamin P. Thomas, wrote in 1950: "Influence is often an unmeasurable, intangible quality, but in whatever degree Weld influenced Mrs. Stowe, through her he moved the world."

Free blacks were a crucial element in the abolitionist movement. Many belonged to antislavery societies and more than a few served as effective speakers both here and abroad. A number were associated with the Underground Railway, which we shall mention later.

The most famous of the Negro abolitionist leaders was Frederick Douglass. As a young man, he made an extemporaneous speech at an antislavery meeting in Nantucket, Massachusetts. On the strength of this the American Antislavery Society hired him as an agent. His commanding appearance and eloquence made the stories he told about his life almost unbelievable. But his autobiography, which appeared in 1845, dispelled all doubts. Slave narratives were common and sometimes not accurate, but Douglass's proved to be authentic and became a classic. He spent two years in England and Ireland and while abroad came to the realization that emancipation could bring the black man economic opportunity and social equality. For 17 years Douglass edited the antislavery *North Star* in Rochester, New York. Unlike Garrison, he believed in the power of political action and allied himself with James Birney. During the Civil War, Douglass would recruit blacks, among them his own sons, for the Union Army.

In 1839 the American Antislavery Society was split in two because of disagreement over Garrison's policies, including the issue of women's rights. The element that withdrew was led by Lewis Tappan, James Birney, and Henry Stanton. The new organization that they founded was known as the American and Foreign Antislavery Society. Neither society had the effectiveness of the original one, and the division weakened the abolitionist movement. Also, many free blacks resented the racism and paternalism of the whites and preferred to focus their efforts by holding all-black Negro conventions.

According to historian Larry Gara, a blend of fiction and fact characterizes the so-called Underground Railway. Obviously, the closer the slave to a free state, the better his chances of escape. Very rarely did an abolitionist venture into the South to encourage escape; help, therefore, was more available in the border and northern states. In general, abolitionists provided shelter, food, and clothes, and they often furnished wagons to transport "passengers" to the next "station." Also, they usually had the names of others who could be

Frederick Douglass, c. 1817–1895. Courtesy Schomburg Center for Research in Black Culture, New York Public Library.

trusted. As mentioned, although the free states had no slave codes, there was the danger that a fugitive could be apprehended, legally, by agents of the master. In Canada, the slave was safe.

To reach freedom, the slave almost always had to make his own plans and depend on his own initiative. This required great courage and physical stamina as well as resourcefulness. He had to hide out, live off the land, and walk for very long distances, usually at night. Otherwise he had to obtain transportation of some type — wagon, railway, riverboat or coastal vessel — going north. He sometimes stole horses, "free" papers, money (as did Cassy), or whatever was needed. But many men and women made successful escapes, some even from the deep South. How many did run away? One clue is the 1850 census. Out of a slave population of over three million, roughly 1,000 slaves were missing and presumed to be fugitives.

According to an early authority on the Underground Railway, the term "underground" was used in 1831 when railroads were beginning to gain attention. He cites an instance when a slave escaped across the Ohio River from Kentucky and disappeared on the Ohio side, causing the pursuing master to say, "That nigger must have gone off on an underground road."

Uncle Tom's Cabin thrills its readers with escapes of the Harrises and of Emmeline and Cassy. Harriet's descriptions bring to mind the real life escape of Ellen and William Craft, mentioned in the *Liberator* in 1849. Ellen had inherited a very light complexion from her father, who was her owner. (Harriet's escaping characters were also light.) William Craft was a skilled cabinetmaker and was able to save enough money for them to get from Macon, Georgia, to Philadelphia. Ellen posed as an ailing southern gentleman with one arm in a sling (she could not write, and this ruse excused her from signing such things as hotel registers). William acted as his (her) personal servant. They traveled first class in trains and steamboats and stopped at good hotels without arousing suspicion. They learned from a free black of an abolitionist in Philadelphia who would aid them. They lived in Boston but later fled to England to avoid capture.

The most famous "conductor" was probably Harriet Tubman, herself an escaped slave. She is credited with returning to the South 19 times to lead to freedom more than 300 slaves, including members of her family. Two "stationmasters" of note are the Quaker Levi Coffin of Newport, Indiana, who aided the escape of more than 300, and John Rankin, the Ohio minister whose home in Ripley was a refuge for Kentucky slaves crossing the Ohio. (Coffin is represented by Harriet's Simeon Halliday, and Harriet may have heard from Rankin a story about a slave mother escaping across the ice floes of the Ohio River.) John Fairfield, the son of a Virginia slaveholder, was one "conductor" who did venture south to arrange escapes, delivering the blacks to Coffin or going with them to Canada. Historians agree that the existence of the underground enraged Southerners and tended to cause harsher and more restrictive treatment of slaves and free blacks.

Although the abolitionists were unyielding in their demand for immediate emancipation, they did not agree on what was meant by immediate. This caused great confusion. It should be noted, also, that their states would not have to deal with mass liberation or the economic problems involved, and they did not concern themselves to any extent with the issue of exploitation of labor in their own North. Most abolitionists came from New England, although some were transplanted Southerners. Many were clergy of evangelical churches, but there were also many lay members, most of whom had intense religious commitment. By 1850 membership in Abolitionist societies had reached a total of about 150,000. But certainly a larger number of the total population than this disapproved of slavery. New York's William Seward, Lincoln's Secretary of State-to-be, wrote in 1845:

> It is not in human nature that all who desire the abolition of slavery should be inflamed with equal zeal, and different degrees of fervor produce different opinions concerning the measures proper to be adopted.

Harriet, like many others holding strong antislavery sentiments, never formally allied herself with an organized abolitionist group. In 1837 she wrote to Calvin:

> Today I read in Mr. Birney's Philanthropist. Abolitionism being the fashion here [at the home of brother William, in Putnam, Ohio], it is natural to look at its papers.
> It does seem to me that there needs to be an intermediate society. If not, as light increases, all the excesses of the abolition party will not prevent humane and conscientious men from joining it.
> Pray, what is there in Cincinnati to satisfy one whose mind is awakened on this subject? No one can have the system of slavery brought before him without an irrepressible desire to do something, and what is there to be done?

Although the non-Garrison abolitionists were turning toward political action, beginning in 1836 free debate on slavery was limited in the House of Representatives because of the so-called gag rules, passed by Southerners and northern Democrats. By 1840 the following was a standing rule (and would remain so until 1844):

> That upon presentation of any memorial or petition praying for the abolition of slavery or the slave trade in any District, Territory, or State of the Union, and upon the presentation of any resolution, or other paper touching that subject, the *reception* of such memorial, petition, resolution, or paper, shall be considered as objected to, and the *question of its reception* shall be laid on the table, without debate, or further action thereon.
> That no petition, memorial, resolution, or other paper praying for the abolition of slavery in the District of Columbia, or any State or Territory, or the slave trade between the States or Territories of the United States in which it now exists, shall be received by this House, or entertained in any way whatever.

John Quincy Adams, 1767–1848. Portrait by Brady c. 1845. Courtesy National Archives.

The fight against this was led by John Quincy Adams, who had served as the sixth president and was elected to the House in 1831. Adams's past record showed that he was no abolitionist, and he does not appear to have considered himself as such. In 1839 he proposed to the House a resolution for a constitutional amendment providing that every child born in the United States after July 4, 1842, should be free, and that neither slave trading nor slavery should exist in the District of Columbia after July 4, 1845. The gag rules effectively blocked discussion of this proposed amendment. However, the proposal shows that while Adams conceded that the Constitution recognized slavery and that slavery would be extended with the admission of Florida (the latter particularly obnoxious to the abolitionists), his aim was the gradual extinction of bondage in the United States. Adams argued that the gag rules violated the First Amendment. He waged a courageous and brilliant campaign against them, refusing to obey them and presenting forbidden petitions from constituents.

Petitions had been effective in the British antislavery campaign and the Americans realized their importance, using them to ask, for example, emancipation in the nation's capital, prohibition of the annexation of Texas, prohibition of slavery in the territories, and probition of the domestic slave trade. After the adoption of the first gag rule, the American Antislavery Society organized a drive to flood Congress with petitions. John Greenleaf Whittier, the poet, was involved in this, and between January, 1837, and March, 1838, the society presented more than 400,000. Most of these had been circulated by women. The instructions sent to petitioners are interesting:

> Let petitions be circulated wherever signers can be got. Neglect no one. Follow the farmer to his field, the wood chopper to the forest. Hail the shopkeeper behind his counter; call the clerk from his desk; stop the waggoner with his team; forget not the matron, ask for her daughter. Let no frown deter, no repulse baffle. Explain, discuss, argue, persuade.

Supporting Adams were William Slade of Vermont and Joshua Giddings of Ohio, and in 1841 the American Antislavery Society called Weld to Washington to work behind the scenes as a researcher and assistant in the fight for the right of petition. In 1844, when he was 77, Adams succeeded in bringing about the repeal of the gag rules; so the congressional "conspiracy of silence" was broken.

There were other signs that the fight against slavery was becoming political: In 1837, at the age of 28, Abraham Lincoln made an official protest against slavery, requesting that the same be recorded in the *House Journal* of the Illinois Legislature.

Abolitionists less inflexible than Garrison shunned political action because it meant compromise with principles. But pragmatism won out, and such abolitionists formed an antislavery party. James Birney, the ex-slaveholder, became in 1840 the presidential candidate for the newly formed Liberty Party. He received only 7,000 votes in that election, but claimed more than 60,000 in 1840. The Free Soil Party gradually superceded the Liberty Party. The last was formed to keep slavery out of the territories recently acquired from Mexico. Its leader was Joshua Leavitt, editor and an active member of the American Antislavery Society. The first candidate, Martin Van Buren (who had served as the eighth president), took 156,000 votes in 1848. By 1854 the former Free Soilers had joined the new, antislavery Republican Party, which consisted of various Northerners.

One of those instrumental in organizing the Republican Party was Charles Sumner of Massachusetts, who from 1851 until his death in 1874 served as that state's senator in Washington. In 1849 he had as a lawyer challenged the legality of segregated schools in Boston. A superb orator, he had a real hatred of slavery—a hatred so deep that he even supported compensating slave owners at national expense. (This was contrary to abolitionist principles.) As a senator he pressed unrelentingly for emancipation and, after adoption of the Thirteenth Amendment, for racial equality. His party's first successful presidential candidate was, of course, Abraham Lincoln.

Charles Sumner, 1811–1874. Courtesy Schomburg Center for Research in Black Culture, New York Public Library.

5

The Exploited Sex

But I suffer not a woman to teach, nor to usurp authority, but to be in silence.

— *St. Paul (I Timothy 2:12)*

The first duty, I believe, which devolves on our sex now is to think for ourselves....

— *Sarah Grimké, 1837*

The author of *Uncle Tom* was a woman, and the book's American readership included thousands of women. With this in mind, we shall look at the lives of white women in antebellum America.

The nation's 1850 census showed a population of slightly more than 23 million. The long-settled New England states had a surplus of women; California, representing the frontier, had a surplus of men. Although more than half of the population still made their living in agriculture, the country was becoming more urbanized.

In colonial times, the scarcity of women had emphasized their importance. By mid-nineteenth century, women in Victorian America were generally reduced to dependency status, though there were marked regional and class differences. In the South, wives and daughters of wealthy plantation owners were put on a pedestal, supposedly shielded and protected from realities; they were waited on and not expected to do menial work in their own homes. Harriet shows this by expressing the scorn of St. Clare's servants when Miss Ophelia actually does housework. (However, on plantations Southern women often nursed the sick and had important supervisory duties, as we have seen on page 67.) She also shows that earning money in the home was frowned upon: As Mrs. Shelby considers taking music pupils to raise money to buy back Tom, Mr.

Shelby comments, "You wouldn't degrade yourself that way, Emily. I would never consent to it." When a man and wife worked together to maintain a farm, there was recognition of the fact that the woman's labor was needed for survival. But when the husband left home every day to work at a business or industry, the wife lost independence. Although she worked very hard at home, her labor was considered much less productive than her husband's, presumably because she received no financial recompense. Such a woman was her husband's dependent rather than his partner, and in almost all families the husband's (or father's or brother's) word was law.

If a woman had to or chose to support herself, where could she work and still be considered a lady? Aside from writing at home, teaching the very young was a respectable occupation, and one not particularly attractive to men. In fact, Catherine Beecher, Harriet's sister, noted that male aversion to this profession was to be expected when the "excitement and profits of commerce, manufactures, agriculture, and the arts" were available. By 1850 elementary education was a primary responsibility of most states except those in the South. The requirements to teach in public or private schools were minimal, and, as would be expected, the pay was poor. Other possibilities for low-paid work were domestic service, sewing, and factory work. Women who did such work were not considered ladies, despite the necessity that drove nearly all of them to out-of-the-house labor.

Although small numbers of women worked in the marketplace, Victorian attitudes encouraged them to stay at home. According to one female writer:

> That *home* is her [woman's] appropriate and appointed sphere of action there cannot be a shadow of doubt; for the dictates of nature are plain and imperative on the subject, and the injunctions given in Scripture are no less explicit.

For those not familiar with Scripture:

> Unto the woman he [God] said, I will greatly multiply thy sorrow and thy conception; in sorrow thou shalt bring forth children; and thy desire shall be to thy husband, and he shall rule over thee. (Genesis 3:16)
> Wives, submit yourselves unto your own husbands, as unto the Lord. For the husband is the head of the wife, even as Christ is the head of the church.... (Ephesians 5:22,23)

So most middle-class young women from both rural and urban areas stayed at home until they married. They learned cooking and dressmaking, abilities that would serve them well as future housewives. (But of their sexual roles in marriage, they were taught nothing.) Women at home also knitted and made hooked rugs; they painted, played the harp or piano, and sang. They also gardened.

By the 1830s higher education of sorts was available in the women's colleges of the East, such as Mount Holyoke, or at the coeducational colleges west of the Appalachians. Few women, however, were in a position to attend such institutions. Lucy Stone, the feminist, graduated from Oberlin College in 1847, but "every employment was closed to me, except those of the teacher, the seamstress, and the housekeeper." Medicine was virtually a closed profession, and the first medical degree awarded in the United States to a woman was granted in 1849 by an institution for men. (The Women's Medical College of Pennsylvania was opened in 1850 to circumvent this.) The situation was similar in the legal profession. It was not until after the Civil War that the first schools of nursing were founded in this country. Secretarial work was in the future, the first typewriters being placed on the market in the 1870s. A teacher of the era wrote: "There was only one avenue open ... marriage." And as late as 1873 a Supreme Court opinion stated that "the paramount destiny and mission of a woman is to fulfill [*sic*] the noble and benign office of wife and mother. This is the law of the Creator."

Common law, adopted from the British, held that married women had neither property nor money of their own; a wife's inheritance — even her wages — belonged to her husband. Between 1839 and the end of the nineteenth century, every state enacted laws to improve this situation. Unfortunately, these laws varied greatly and judges emphasized that the common law prevailed unless statute ruled otherwise. It is interesting to note that marriage was regarded as legalized prostitution by feminist Mary Wollstonecraft, who died before Harriet was born, and by birth control advocate Margaret Sanger, whose day came after Harriet's death.

The following shows the hypocrisy of the southern woman's position. Mary Boykin Chesnut, who lived on plantations as daughter and wife, wrote in 1861:

> Mrs. Stowe did not hit the sorest spot. She makes Legree a bachelor.... And I knew the dissolute half of Legree well. He was high and mighty, but the

kindest creature to his slaves. And the unfortunate results of his bad ways were not sold, and had not to jump over ice blocks. They were kept in full view and provided for handsomely in his will.

The wife and daughters in the might of their purity and innocence are supposed never to dream of what is as plain before their eyes as the sunlight, and they play their parts as unsuspecting angels to the letter.

With regard to the double standard in sex, at least some northern women endeavored to do something about it. The New York Magdalen Society in 1832 had reported that 10,000 prostitutes lived and worked in New York City. By 1834 the New York Female Moral Reform Society had been formed, and a drive against prostitution begun. Besides trying to reform the fallen women, the reformers tackled wayward men:

We think it proper even to expose names, for the same reason that the names of thieves and robbers are published, that the public may know them and govern themselves accordingly. We mean to let the licentious know, that if they are not ashamed of their debasing vice, we will not be ashamed to expose them....

Names did appear in the *Advocate*, the society's publication.

The women of farm families often raised their own wool and flax to make clothes for their families. They butchered animals, milked, made butter and cheese, and raised fruits and vegetables to preserve. They also made candles and soap.

On the frontier, life was harsh for both men and women. Whether the pioneer wife lived in a log cabin in the forest or in a sod house in the plains, she led a life of unceasing toil and usually isolation. Her lot is well described by Alexis de Tocqueville, who visited the United States in the 1830s:

To devote herself to austere duties, submit herself to privations which were unknown to her, embrace an existence for which she was not made, such was the occupation of the finest years of her life, such have been for her the delights of marriage. Want, suffering and loneliness have affected her constitution, but now bowed her courage. Mid the profound sadness painted on her delicate features, you may easily remark a religious resignation and profound peace....

Men and women who made the trek west often died on the way. In the account of his overland journey to California in search of gold,

Alonzo Delano tells of a woman in a wagon train near the North Fork of the Platte River (which flows through the present states of Wyoming and Nebraska):

> By degrees the opinion was formed that [her husband] was murdered, and she left among strangers, upon a barren wilderness, with her two helpless children, with a long, doubtful and dangerous journey before her and all the uncertainty of an unsettled and barbarous country on her arrival in California, if she should be so fortunate as to reach it herself.

He goes on to say that this woman settled in California's Feather River basin, which was known as a rich source of gold in the mid-1800s. To support herself she ran a hotel and later became housekeeper for a Dr. Willoughby. But within a short time she was dead, "leaving her children to Dr. Willoughby's care."

The wife who lived in a town or city—and this would include Harriet—led a very different life. She did not grow the food for her table nor weave the cloth for her clothes. She lacked modern conveniences such as central heating, electric regrigerator, thermostated stove, vacuum cleaner, washer, dryer and permanent press materials. (The sewing machine, however, began to be mass produced in 1851.) The weekly washing and ironing were not only time-consuming but often required considerable labor. There were tasks unknown today: fires to be made and grates to be cleaned; lamps to be cleaned and wicks to be trimmed. On the other hand, domestic help could be hired for a pittance.

The housewife was not even comfortably dressed. Corsets fashioned of silk or cotton and ribbed with whale bone or steel stays were in vogue. These contraptions extended from chest to hips and their effect on the figure could be controlled by adjustable lacings. Hoop skirts with skeletons of steel or whalebone and measuring sometimes as much as five feet in diameter at the hem were also worn. (Note Harriet's skirt in the family portrait on page 130.)

Here are some instructions from *The Frugal Housewife*, written in 1829 by Lidia Maria Child (Harriet was probably of necessity a frugal housewife):

> When mattresses get hard and bunchy, rip them, take the hair out, pull it thoroughly by hand, let it lie a day or two to air, wash the tick, lay it in as light and even as possible, and catch it down, as before. Thus prepared, they will be as good as new.

If feather-beds smell badly, or become heavy, from want of proper preservation of the feathers, or from old age, empty them, and wash the feathers thoroughly in a tub of suds; spread them in your garret to dry, and they will be as light and as good as new.

Keep a coarse broom for the cellar stairs, wood-shed, yard, &c. No good housekeeper allows her carpet broom to be used for such things.

After old coats, pantaloons, &c. have been cut up for boys, and are no longer capable of being converted into garments, cut them into strips, and employ the leisure moments of children, or domestics, in sewing and braiding them for door-mats.

In winter, always set the handle of your pump as high as possible before you go to bed. Except in very frigid weather, this keeps the handle from freezing. When there is reason to apprehend extreme cold, do not forget to throw a rug or horse-blanket over the pump; a frozen pump is a comfortless preparation for a winter's breakfast.

Never allow ashes to be taken up in wood, or put into wood. Always have your tinder-box and lantern ready for use, in case of sudden alarm. Have important papers all together, where you can lay your hand on them at once, in case of fire.

If a woman had time for reading, she could turn for advice to the magazine *Godey's Lady Book*. Advice from all quarters emphasized the necessity of discipline in childraising; the following is typical:

It requires only a little firmness in the beginning ... to make children conform to the dictates of their parents, and to render them entirely obedient to their wills; for it is only necessary to commence sufficiently early, to make the child know it is not to think for itself. — W.P. Dewees, 1838.

Women were supposed to be more spiritual and more pure than men, and thus the character of the child was the responsibility of the mother.

Poets such as Longfellow, Holmes, and Whittier were read. Dickens was highly regarded, but writers such as Hawthorne, Melville, Whitman, Poe, and Thoreau, admired today, were not particularly popular. Poe, for example, was known to be a heavy drinker, and it was held that no artist of questionable character was likely to produce works meeting the era's standards of good taste. The housewife was more likely to prefer a sentimental novel by one of what Hawthorne termed "a d——d mob of scribbling women."

In 1860 the average number of children borne by an American woman was 5.1; not all of these reached maturity, however. An 1845 census of Boston revealed shocking infant and maternal death rates, and there is no reason to believe that health problems were worse in Boston than in other parts of the nation. Knowledge about communicable diseases, sanitation, and nutrition was scanty, with the result that deaths at all ages were commonplace and people lived in an atmosphere of continuing uncertainty as to whether their offspring or they themselves might be struck down.

Moralists claimed that marriage should produce children. Doubtless many couples wished to limit the number of these children, but effective contraceptive methods were little known or practiced. However, the widely read advice of Sylvester Graham, a Presbyterian minister and reformer and for whom a type of flour is named, might have, if followed, prevented a few births. Believing the current theory of his day that one ounce of semen equaled about 40 ounces of blood, Graham advocated that husbands remain robust by having sexual intercourse no more than 12 times a year. Many women must have desired infrequent intercourse, if only for the reason that it could mean fewer babies and fewer deaths from childbirth.

If a woman wanted a divorce, could she get it? First and foremost, attitudes were against it. As late as 1880, a Philadelphia minister said in a speech:

> Wifehood is the crowning glory of a woman. In it she is bound for all time. To her husband she owes the duty of unqualified obedience. There is no crime which a man can commit which justifies his wife in leaving him or applying for that monstrous thing, divorce. It is her duty to subject herself to him always, and no crime he can commit can justify her lack of disobedience. Let divorce be anathema; curse it, curse it!

Despite the social stigma of divorce, it was legal in some states but only on grounds of bigamy, adultery, impotence, desertion, and extreme cruelty. As early as 1824, however, Indiana accepted any "just and reasonable grounds"; it would be many decades before all states would enact similar legislation. In most cases a divorced wife was dependent on the husband's inclination to provide support and even grant child custody. Elizabeth Cady Stanton was unflagging in her efforts to bring before the public the need for liberal divorce laws.

The abolitionist movement claimed the energy of many capable women. Later some of these women would use the experience so gained to fight for women's rights.

Maria Weston Chapman in 1832 formed an auxiliary to

Garrison's New England Antislavery Society. The Boston Female Antislavery Society, as it was called, ran yearly antislavery fairs which proved to be successful fund raisers. Beginning in 1839, Mrs. Chapman and her sister edited *The Liberty Bell*, an annual gift book to which well-known abolitionists from here and abroad contributed. Later Maria initiated petition campaigns.

Lidia Maria Child, the author whose household advice we have just quoted, was the wife of an antislavery publisher. She was also a recognized author and a Garrison devotee. In 1833 she wrote *An Appeal on Behalf of That Class of Americans Called Africans*, distinguished by its condemnation of northern racial prejudice. Lidia, like Maria Chapman, was a Unitarian.

Lucretia Mott of Philadelphia was a Quaker minister. She and her husband James were both teachers and had involved themselves in antislavery activities since 1820. As mentioned, she was invited (belatedly) to the founding meetings of the American Antislavery Society in 1833; soon afterward she formed the Philadelphia Female Antislavery Society. Her emphasis was on the importance of following one's conscience, and it is not surprising that after the 1850 fugitive slave law was enacted, she and James allowed runaway slaves to remain in their home.

Lucy Stone, another Garrison follower and mentioned earlier, managed to work her way through Oberlin College, graduating in 1847 at the age of 28. The next year saw her a lecturer for the Massachusetts Antislavery Society, discussing not only the plight of the slave, but that of what she considered another type of slave, woman.

Ten years earlier, the idea of a female lecturer had caused great controversy. The person involved was Angelina Grimké. Angelina and her older sister Sarah were members of a rich and distinguished South Carolina family of slaveholders. Both women had come to despise slavery and had left the South, Sarah in 1822 and Angelina seven years later. Deeply religious and zealous of doing good, they had joined the Society of Friends and settled in Philadelphia. By 1835 Angelina was a member of Lucretia Mott's female antislavery society, which included free black women. But that summer, when whites in Philadelphia rioted against blacks, she became aware of the racial tension that existed in the North.

In fact, violence was on the rise in many parts of the North. Worse still, municipal and other authorities offered very little protection or support to blacks or to abolitionists. The organized churches were showing more and more opposition to immediatism. Even the women involved were in danger: For example, Prudence Crandall of Canterbury, Connecticut was threatened and insulted, suffered damage to her property, and was finally tried for violation of a state law when she started a boarding school for colored girls. When George Thompson, the aggressive British antislavery leader, came to the United States on behalf of the abolitionist cause, he was mobbed at every turn. Americans at this time had great antipathy for the English, and this, plus the fact that Thompson was a friend of Garrison, made his position intolerable. One minister thought that Thompson "had no business in this country stirring up trouble." Most people seemed to apply this reasoning to all the abolitionists.

The Liberator kept Angelina informed of the various persecutions suffered by the abolitionists. On August 30, 1835 she wrote to Garrison, encouraging him to persevere. Here are some sentences from her letter:

> The ground upon which you stand is holy ground: never—never surrender it. If you surrender it, the hope of the slave is extinguished, and the chains of his servitude is strengthened a hundred fold.... If persecution is the means which God has ordained for the accomplishment of this great end, EMANCIPATION, then, in dependence upon Him for strength to bear it, I feel as if I could say, LET IT COME; for it is my deep, solemn, deliberate conviction, that this is a cause worth dying for.

To write such a letter to the radical Garrison, of whom probably her Quaker friends and certainly her family disapproved, must have required considerable courage. Garrison published the letter in its entirety. Angelina next wrote a pamphlet entitled *An Appeal to the Christian Women of the South*, urging them to overthrow slavery. Authorities in her home state burned copies of the appeal and threatened her with prison if she returned to South Carolina. Angelina, in common with many Quakers, had great interest in promoting "free" products (not involved with slave labor) and hoped for support in this enterprise, but she received little encouragement.

The American Antislavery Society wanted to capitalize on the fact that an aristocratic southern woman was championing its cause. Thus it was that Angelina was invited to come to New York to be trained as one of the 70. Sarah, who had gradually accepted immediatism, went with her. Sarah was then 44 and Angelina 31. The women were trained by Weld and others experienced in lecturing,

mob control, and the like. The Grimkés would accept no salary and
paid their own expenses. In a short time they were depicting the evils
of slavery to large audiences of women, usually in church buildings.
Besides speaking in New York City, they traveled to other parts of
New York state and to New Jersey. The following year they attended
the Antislavery Convention of American Women in New York City.
Angelina had been shocked to find racial prejudice prevalent among
the northern abolitionists, and she brought this to the attention of the
convention:

> Our people have erected a false standard by which to judge man's char-
> acter. Because in the slave-holding States colored men are plundered and
> kept in abject ignorance, are treated with disdain and scorn, so here, too in
> profound deference to the South, we refuse to eat, or ride, or walk, or as-
> sociate, or open our institutions of learning, or even our zoological in-
> stitutions to people of color, unless they visit them in the capacity of *ser-
> vants*, of menials in humble attendance upon the Anglo-American. Who
> ever heard of a more wicked absurdity in a Republican country?
>
> Women ought to feel a peculiar sympathy in the colored man's wrong,
> for, like him, she has been accused of mental inferiority, and denied the
> privileges of a liberal education.

Here we see a suggestion of what would become the "woman
question."

At the time, it was customary that women did not address
"promiscuous audiences," which merely meant audiences containing
both sexes; exceptions sometimes included Quaker and Methodist
women. From the beginning there had been some misgivings about
the Grimkés giving talks or lectures in places other than private
homes. The American Antislavery Society did not wish the sisters'
work to be considered in the same unfavorable light as Fanny
Wright's. (Francis Wright was a Scottish reformer who had founded
an ill-fated colony for blacks in Tennessee. She was also an out-
spoken advocate of birth control, sexual freedom, divorce, and equal
rights for women.) Weld, on the other hand, appears to have had no
objection to the Grimkés addressing males. (When working with
the revivalist Finney, he had himself urged women to speak at
meetings.) At any rate, he encouraged the sisters to accept an invitation from Garrison's Female Antislavery Society of Boston to address
New England audiences, which, it transpired, included men.

Angelina and Sarah began their lecturing in June, 1837. They
remained in Massachusetts almost a year, living in the homes of

abolitionists. Sometimes men slipped into the meetings; once in a crowd of about 600 there were some 50 men. Their first large mixed audience — more than 1,000 — was in Lynn, only two weeks after they had arrived. Soon all their audiences were "promiscuous." From various records we know that Angelina was an excellent speaker. (Sarah was not, and after a while Weld requested her not to lecture.) Samuel May, a Garrison abolitionist, was at first critical of Angelina. But after the Grimkés had visited his parish for a week, he changed his mind. According to his *Recollections*, "I never heard from other lips, male or female, such eloquence as that of her closing appeal. The experience of that week dispelled my Pauline prejudice." The sisters had learned from Weld how to counter arguments against immediatism. When they were criticized as women out of their appointed sphere, they began to speak up for the rights of their sex.

One who objected to their role as public reformers was Catherine Beecher, who supported colonization. She had publicly censured Angelina for involving women in the radical abolitionist movement. Miss Beecher believed that women should obey St. Paul's injunctions. "Men," she contended, "are the proper persons to make appeals to the rulers whom they appoint." (Curiously, Catherine Beecher made significant contributions to progressive education for women, although she held that woman's sphere was the home.) Angelina responded in a series of articles that appeared in antislavery publications, and her arguments are representative of feminism.

> Now, I believe it is a woman's right to have a voice in all the laws and regulations by which she is governed, whether in Church or State; and that the present arrangements of society, on these points, are a *violation of human rights, a rank usurpation of power*, a violent seizure and confiscation of what is sacredly and inalienably hers.... If Ecclesiastical and Civil governments are ordained of God, *then* I contend that woman has just as much right to sit in solemn counsel in Conventions, Conferences, Associations, and General assemblies, as man — just as much right to sit upon the throne of England, or in the Presidential Chair of the United States.... The discussion of the rights of the slave has opened the way for the discussion of other rights, and the ultimate result will most certainly be the breaking of *every* yoke, the letting the oppressed of every grade and description go free, — an emancipation far more glorious than any the world has ever yet seen....

Sarah was also writing a series on the equality of the sexes. Here is an excerpt:

That there is a root of bitterness continually springing up in families and troubling the repose of both men and women, must be manifest to even a superficial observer; and I believe it is the mistaken notion of the inequality of the sexes. As there is an assumption of superiority on the one part, which is not sanctioned by Jehovah, there is an incessant struggle on the other to rise to that degree of dignity, which God designed women to possess in common with men, and to maintain those rights and exercise those privileges which every woman's common sense, apart from the prejudices of education, tells her are inalienable; they are a part of her moral nature, and can only cease when her immortal mind is extinguished.

On July 28, 1837, the General Association of Congregational Ministers of Massachusetts issued a pastoral letter relative to the activities of the Grimkés. They were not named, but the reference was clear:

[The church should not permit] strangers to preach on subjects the ministers do not agree with.... [Women should exercise their] appropriate duties and influence ... as clearly stated in the New Testament.... The power of woman is her dependence. But when she assumes the place and tone of man as a public reformer, our care and protection of her seems unnecessary.... If the vine, whose strength and beauty is to lean upon the trelliswork, and half conceal its clusters, thinks to assume the independence and the overshadowing nature of the elm, it will not only cease to bear fruit, but fall in shame and dishonour into the dust.

But the lecturing to promiscuous assemblies continued, and with greater and greater success. Garrison, with his belief in sexual equality, was elated. However, the sisters found a communication from Weld more disconcerting than the pastoral letter. He wrote:

What is done for the slave and human rights in this country must be done now, now, now. Delay is madness, ruin, whereas woman's rights are not a life and death business, now or never. Why can't you have eyes to see this? The wayfaring man, though a fool, need not err here, it is so plain. What will you run a tilt at next?

The last sentence probably referred to Garrison's propensity for involving himself in all manner of reforms, a practice of which Weld vehemently disapproved. Whittier also wrote to caution:

You are now doing much and nobly to vindicate and assert the rights of women. Your lectures to crowded and promiscuous audiences ... are practical and powerful assertions of the right and duty of woman to labor side by side with her brother for the welfare and redemption of the world. Why, then, let me ask, is it necessary for you to enter the lists as controversial writers on this question? Does it not look, dear sisters, like abandoning in some degree the cause of the poor and miserable slave?

The Grimkés' public careers ended with Angelina's marriage to Weld in Philadelphia in 1838. Concommitant with the wedding were the opening ceremonies of the new $40,000 Pennsylvania Hall, built by abolitionists and dedicated to free speech. Two days later more than 3,000 immediatists were at an evening meeting in the hall. A noisy and unruly crowd outside broke windows by hurling bricks and stones. Angelina spoke for more than an hour, disregarding the turmoil. Following her was a young Quaker named Abbey Kelley. Weld was so impressed by Miss Kelley that he strongly encouraged her to continue lecturing for abolitionism. (This she did—and in a way, it was to her that Angelina passed on the torch.) Before the night was out, the mob had burned down Pennsylvania Hall, with the mayor and fire department lending little help.

Thus Angelina's relatively short but influential speaking career ended abruptly. Weld never resumed his lecturing either. Why these two unusually talented orators elected to work backstage is not known. (Weld's voice had suffered seriously from his public speaking, but it is possible that he had other reasons for retirement.) The Grimkés had great affection for Garrison and his followers; Weld was aligned with the Tappans, Birney, and others of the New York group, and soon their differences with Garrison became irreconcilable—to the detriment of the abolitionist movement.

But the "woman question" did not disappear from abolitionist circles. It came up again at the World Antislavery Convention in London. Lucretia Mott was there, as was Henry Stanton with his bride, Elizabeth Cady Stanton. But women had no vote in the proceedings. Mrs. Stanton recorded her contact with Mrs. Mott:

The acquaintance of Lucretia Mott, who was a broad, liberal thinker on politics, religion, and all questions of reform, opened to me a new world of thought. As we walked about to see the sights of London, I embraced every opportunity to talk with her. It was intensely gratifying to hear all that, through years of doubt, I had dimly thought, so freely discussed.... As Mrs. Mott and I walked home, arm in arm, commenting on the incidents of the day, we resolved to hold a convention as soon as we returned home, and form a society to advance the rights of women.

The meeting they envisaged took place at Seneca Falls, New York, in 1848, and began the movement for women's rights and suffrage. Following the Civil War, when black males were to be granted the vote, Susan B. Anthony (who had worked as an antislavery agent) tried in vain to have that right extended to all women. But most people agreed with the view of Frederick Douglass:

> When women, because they are women, are dragged from their homes and hung upon lamp-posts; when their children are torn from their arms and their brains dashed to the pavement; when they are objects of insult and outrage at every turn; when they are in danger of having their homes burnt down over their heads; when their children are not allowed to enter schools; then they will have an urgency to obtain the ballot.

But in 1876 the *New York Herald* reported the following: At the Republican Convention, meeting in Cincinnati, a Mrs. Sarah Spencer, who was a delegate of the National Women's Suffrage Association, asked Douglass how he justified speaking the previous day about the continuing plight of his race, while at the same time failing to say a word for American women. She added that to a woman—Harriet Beecher Stowe—he and his people owed more than to any body of men or to any political party. Douglass returned that he would have spoken on behalf of women had he thought of it. (As a matter of record, Douglass favored women's rights.) Women did not obtain the vote until the Nineteenth Amendment was passed in 1920. Blacks and women are still seeking equality.

Where was Harriet while Lucretia Mott, Lidia Child, the Grimkés, and the rest were fighting for the slave? In 1836 she married Calvin Stowe and within a year gave birth to twins. For some time to come, her energy would be concentrated on her growing family. But this experience brought one of her triumphs; *Uncle Tom* succeeded in making the white mother identify with the black mother.

When *Uncle Tom's Cabin* was published in book form, the review in the *Southern Literary Messenger* contained this, among other criticisms:

> We know that among other novel doctrines in vogue in the land of Mrs. Stowe's nativity—the pleasant land of New England—which we are old-fashioned enough to condemn, is one which would place a woman on a footing of political equality with men, and causing her to look beyond the office for which she was created—the high and holy office of maternity—would engage her in the administration of public affairs; thus handing over

the State to the perilous protection of diaper diplomatists and wet-nurse politicians. Mrs. Stowe, we believe, belongs to this school of Women's Rights, and on this ground she may assert her prerogative to teach us how wicked are we ourselves and the Constitution under which we live. But such a claim is in direct conflict with the letter of scripture, as we find it recorded in the second chapter of the First Epistle to Timothy....

6

Harriet's Era

We are great, and rapidly ... growing. This is our pride and danger, our weakness and strength....
— *John C. Calhoun, 1817*

Harriet was born in 1811 and died in 1896. However, we shall consider her era the period roughly extending from 1811, when Napoleon was waging a war that indirectly precipitated the war of 1812, until 1865, when Harriet's major work bore fruit in the form of the Thirteenth Amendment to the Constitution. The purpose of this chapter is to orient the reader to this era by briefly reviewing some of its important events, social history, and attitudes.

In 1810 the population of the United States was slightly more than seven million. By 1865 it had increased about five-fold. But even by 1860, five out of six persons still lived on small farms and in small towns and villages. The Napoleonic Wars provided impetus for the industrialization of this country. At first, products as diverse as shoes and pianos were made in households, but gradually the factory system prevailed. Before 1830 the cotton textile industry grew the fastest — for example, by 1840 cotton mills employed 100,000 people. Industries such as the manufacture of firearms, woolens, iron agricultural machinery, shoes, and leather goods expanded also.

Increased productivity in both agriculture and industry led to improved means of transportation. There was a boom in canals. The Eric Canal, completed in 1825, with one terminus the Hudson River and the other Lake Erie, was the most important. This was 363 miles long with 83 locks and was designed for barges at first drawn by horses or mules. Later another canal was built to connect Lake Erie with the Ohio River. This greatly increased commerce between the

Midwest and the east coast; it also contributed significantly to the development of New York City and encouraged the westward migration of many Americans as well as immigrants from Europe. The modern descendant of the Erie Canal is the New York State Barge Canal System. The success of the Erie Canal spurred construction of many other canals; so by 1840 there were more than 3,000 miles of canals, most of them located east of the Mississippi. Passengers in canal boats were subjected to some inconveniences, among them the necessity of going below deck or lying down when the vessel went under a bridge. Canals flourished until superseded by the railway.

The advent of the steamboat was a boon to the Midwest and the South, and by 1830 about 200 steam-powered, shallow draft vessels (similar to the one that took Tom to New Orleans) were plying the Mississippi and its tributaries. These were a vast improvement over the flatboats that could move only downstream. Passengers sometimes demanded more speed than was prudent, and crews of rival vessels were known to race each other, with the result that explosions and other accidents were not uncommon. Night boats proved to be attractive to prostitutes.

Yankee ships carried everything, even ice and whale oil. Ocean trade was carried on mainly by packet, brig, and the faster clipper. In 1851 *The Flying Cloud*, for example, sailed from New York to San Francisco in 89 days. (With no Panama Canal, rounding Cape Horn was necessary.) But even as early as 1838, the steam-packet *Sirius* had made the trip from Cork, Ireland, to New York City in 19 days, and it was clear that steam would ultimately supplant sail in coastal and oceanic waters. (Harriet, by the way, traveled to Europe both by steamship and clipper.) By 1860 American merchant ships were sailing even to Asiatic ports.

In 1830 this country had only 23 miles of railroad track. In ten years this increased more than a hundred-fold, and by mid-century railways were common in the East. The Atlantic and Pacific oceans were permanently linked with the completion of the Union Pacific in 1869. Train travel in its early days left much to be desired; engines burned wood cut along the run; ventilation in cars was poor, as the windows were sealed; at night a single candle might provide lighting for an entire car; and there was no uniform gauge for the rails, with the result that travelers were constantly forced to change cars. At first the average speed was around ten miles per hour, but by 1850 this had increased to about 30. And in that same year, stuffed seats and springs were introduced. When Lincoln went to Gettysburg in 1863, the presidential car was drawn by horses from the tracks of one railway in Baltimore to the tracks of another.

The growth of roads was slow due to the continuing argument over whether local or federal government was responsible for their construction and maintenance. Until the 1830s the huge Conestoga wagon carried many westward-bound families over, for example, the National Road, connecting Maryland and Illinois. The Conestoga was usually pulled by six horses harnessed in pairs, and was capable of holding loads weighing ten tons. The wheels were good in mud and large enough to ford many streams. As westward migration extended beyond the Mississippi, the Conestoga gave way to the faster "prairie schooner." An ordinary farm wagon fitted with a characteristic canvas top, it was often drawn by oxen. To cross rivers, it could be put on a raft constructed on the spot.

Although roads were few in number and primitive, the stage coach was commonly used in various parts of the country between 1800 and 1840. Its team of four or six horses was changed at stages along the journey. As many as 18 passengers could be accommodated, along with baggage, mail, and driver. Inside the coach, the passengers sat on parallel rows of benches, doubtless uncomfortable, for the stages lacked springs. In good weather, a rate of ten miles per hour was possible. Coaches ultimately gave way to the railroad.

Long journeys by stage required overnight accommodations, and for many years these were generally poor. At road inns, several persons sometimes slept in one bed. They were also served abominable food; conditions in the small towns of the South were especially bad. At the other end of the spectrum was Boston's Tremont House, opened in 1829. It offered a single room for each guest with a free cake of soap! This was also the first hotel with extensive plumbing, for it had a battery of eight water closets on the ground floor, and its basement bathrooms had cold running water. The guest rooms had whale oil lamps, not candles, and the public rooms had gaslights. By 1833 a New York hotel even had a steam-powered lift for baggage.

With improvements in transportation came improvements in the postal service and lower rates. By 1847 stamps were in use. (Before that, the recipient of a letter paid the postage.) By 1850 the post offices in even small villages of the East were receiving mail at least once a week.

Westward expansion was related to the slavery issue because of the inevitable decision on whether newly settled regions would be slave or free. As we have seen, the Missouri Compromise allowed the extension of slavery only to the area that is now Arkansas and Oklahoma, while the 1850 Compromise provided that the recently acquired territory comprising the present states of Utah and New Mexico could vote on the matter themselves. Both compromises served to preserve the Union, but antagonism was mounting; the antislavery people felt that slavery was spreading, and they were particularly hostile to the fugitive slave section of the second compromise — the same section so odious to Harriet. A Milwaukee editor, for example, charged that the federal government was seeking "to establish the law of slavery and kidnapping on the free soil of Wisconsin." Orator Edward Everett, soon to be a senator from Massachusetts, wrote this in a letter:

> I asked myself this question when Mr. Webster's speech came out, "Could you as a good citizen assist in carrying out such a law: if you heard the hue and cry after a runaway slave, would you run out of your house and help catch him?" This question I answered to myself in the negative, and so, I fancy, would Mr. W. himself.

(We recall that Harriet's fictional Senator Bird helped Eliza, despite all his rhetoric to the contrary.)

Tension increased with the passage of the Kansas-Nebraska Act in 1854 under the leadership of Stephen Douglas, the Democratic senator from Illinois. An area immediately west of Missouri and Iowa had been declared an Indian Reserve in 1830, but 20 years later farmers were coveting the land and industrialists dreaming of a transcontinental railway that would run through it. The new act repealed the Missouri Compromise and provided that the people in the territories of Nebraska and Kansas, as those in New Mexico and Utah, would vote on the slavery issue when each applied for statehood. Missouri, a slave state, was just east of the Kansas border, but abolitionists were determined that Kansas would not be controlled by proslavery forces. *Uncle Tom's Cabin*, published two years previously, had touched the conscience of many Northerners, and there was a strong effort to help the free-state cause. Harriet herself had been instrumental in obtaining the signatures of more than 3,000 New England clergymen who opposed the Kansas-Nebraska bill. The

New England Emigrant Aid Society was formed to finance the settlement of free-soil people in the Kansas Territory. Other agencies and
persons joined in, and Whittier even provided the emigrants with
words to sing:

> We cross the prairies as of old
> The Pilgrims crossed the sea,
> To make the West, as they the East,
> The homestead of the free.

Most of the new settlers came from the Midwest. There followed
an influx of proslavery people from Missouri especially but also from
Alabama, Georgia, and South Carolina, and the struggle became
more intense.

When the first territorial election was held in 1855, the
proslavery Senator David Atchison of Missouri was responsible for
bribing more than 3,000 men from his state to cross the border to
vote illegally in Kansas. As a result of this ballot-stuffing, eight of 31
members of the Kansas territorial legislature did not belong there.
Backed by President Pierce, this proslavery body did everything
possible to rid Kansas of the antislavery faction. But these free-staters
formed their own territorial government with Lawrence as their
headquarters. They needed breech-loading Sharps rifles, which were
supplied by their supporters in the East. These carbines came to be
known as Beecher's Bibles because some of the money used to
purchase them had been donated by Henry Ward's congregation in
Brooklyn. The situation in Kansas became familiar to other parts of
the country, particularly through the writings of Horace Greeley, the
antislavery editor of the *New York Tribune*, and through speeches of
Charles Sumner, the abolitionist Massachusetts senator mentioned in
Chapter 4.

In 1856 "border ruffians" from Missouri sacked Lawrence. There
was retaliation, the bloodiest occurring under the direction of John
Brown. Brown was an abolitionist and a religious fanatic obsessed
with the belief that his mission was to stamp out slavery. This, of
course, spurred on the proslavery people. Even the presence of the
United States cavalry could not prevent the armed conflicts that
continued until 1861. At that time, Kansas was admitted to the Union
as a free state. Ironically, the constitution of the new state excluded
free blacks. It is realized now that the free-soilers whom the

abolitionists supported were, for the most part, racist white farmers who feared the competition of slave labor in the new land and whose antislavery leanings were based on economics rather than humanitarianism. The conflict over Kansas was a rallying point for the recently formed Republican Party, a testing ground for John Brown's scheme to liberate the slaves, and a prelude to the Civil War.

Of course Kansas was not the only territory affected by westward expansion. During the 1840s there was great impetus to drive for the Pacific. It was encouraged by editor John O'Sullivan, who wrote in 1845 of "our manifest destiny to overspread the continent allotted by Providence for the free development of our yearly multiplying millions...." He estimated that by 1945 the population would be over 250 million (the 1940 census showed the population of continental United States to be around 132 million). Henry David Thoreau expressed this a little differently: "I must walk toward Oregon and not toward Europe." In fact, westward expansion often involved jingoism and a taste for adventure. As immigrants from Europe arrived in ever-increasing numbers, Americans with agricultural interests sought more land. This desire, of course, spelled doom for the Indian, whose interests were subordinated to those of the white man. In a Fourth of July address at Portland, Maine, a clergyman named Sylvester Judd stated: "I think we have dealt worse by the Indians than by the Africans. We exterminate the former; we domesticate the latter. We find the black man a peck of corn a week; we curse the red man with whiskey." In this connection, he referred to manifest destiny as "nothing more than consummate selfishness."

Since 1824 American merchants had managed to get mules and wagons from Independence, Missouri, through Osage and Commanche country to Santa Fe in order to trade their merchandise. Now American settlers were leaving Independence bound for the Oregon Territory whose northern boundary (45th parallel) had been settled by a treaty with the British in 1846. The journey to the coast started in the spring and ordinarily took at least five months. From Independence the Oregon Trail followed the west bank of the Missouri north to the Platte River; beyond Fort Leavenworth the emigrants were in Indian country; in southern Wyoming they had to cross the Rocky Mountains at South Pass and then, in what is now Idaho, follow the Snake River for 800 miles, finally crossing into the Oregon Territory to reach the Willamette Valley. The hardships they encountered were extreme: unmarked or doubtful trails; alkali deserts that exhausted the meager water supplies the emigrants carried; cholera outbreaks. Despite these difficulties, the 1860 census reported Oregon's population at 52,000.

In 1847 the Mormon leader, Brigham Young, led a contingent of followers from Council Bluffs on the Missouri River to the Great Salt region in the Utah Territory. Thousands followed. These Latter-day Saints had suffered severe persecution in the Midwest and wanted a place away from outside influences where they could have their own government. Young, indeed, had intended to settle his band beyond the borders of the United States, but his dream was short-lived; just the next year, Mexico ceded all the West to her conqueror, the United States. An industrious sect, self-sufficient and closely knit, the Latter-day Saints remained in Utah and made the barren land prosper by the use of irrigation. (By 1860, Utah's population had reached 40,000.) However, the Mormon practice of polygamy remained abhorrent to those of other persuasions.

Some wagon trains left the Oregon Trail to take the California Trail across the Nevada Desert, going over the Sierra Nevada Mountains into the Sacramento Valley. By 1845 there were about 700 Americans in California. The discovery of gold in 1848 brought hordes of people — foreigners as well as Americans — so that by 1852 California's population had increased to about 250,000. The shrewd Brigham Young, incidentally, did not permit Mormons to engage in mining. This encouraged agriculture in Utah and kept the Saints from seeking wealth from the minerals that were being discovered in other parts of the West.

By enacting the fugitive slave provision, the federal government clearly supported the slave owner in recovering a slave who had escaped to a free state. The Dred Scott decision, named for the slave in question, involved the status of the slave who accompanied his master into free territory and then returned to a slave state. In 1833 his owner was an Army surgeon who was ordered from Missouri, a slave state, to Rock Island in Illinois. (Slavery was forbidden in Illinois by the Northwest Ordinance of 1878 and also in 1818 by its state constitution.) Scott went with his master into Illinois and also lived with him for roughly four years in territory where slavery was prohibited by the Missouri Compromise. He married another slave purchased by the surgeon, and their first child was born north of the Missouri border. Another surviving child was born later in Missouri, to which the Scotts returned in 1838.

Urged on by abolitionists eager to make a test case, Dred Scott sued for his freedom, basing the case on his residence in Illinois and in the Wisconsin Territory. (He was aided in this by two sons of his original owner.) The case was first tried in Missouri state courts and finally reached the Supreme Court as *Dred Scott vs. Sanford*. (John Sanford of New York was then Scott's owner.) The trial began in January, 1856, and the verdict was announced after the inauguration of the Democrat James Buchanan as president. Five of the nine justices came from south of the Mason-Dixon Line and favored a broad decision that would strike down the antislavery provision of the Missouri Compromise. The ruling was against Scott. Chief Justice Roger Taney's majority opinion noted that the framers of the Constitution regarded Negroes as

> a subordinate and inferior class of beings, who had been subjugated by the dominant race, and, whether emancipated or not, yet remained subject to their authority, and had no rights or privileges but such as those who held the power and the Government might choose to grant them.

He ruled that "the plaintiff in error could not be a citizen of the State of Missouri, within the meaning of the Constitution of the United States, and consequently was not entitled to sue in its courts...." Taney's opinion also reflected the push for a broad decision; it declared the Missouri Compromise unconstitutional and held that when slaves were taken into federal territories, their masters did not lose title. Of course this delighted slaveholders, dismayed slaves, infuriated the antislavery people, and carried the nation closer to war. As for Dred Scott himself, he and his wife and two daughters were finally freed in 1857 through abolitionist efforts. Within four months, Dred died of tuberculosis. Today the Dred Scott case is popularly cited as an example of the fallibility of the Supreme Court.

The dissent between North and South increased over John Brown's raid on the federal arsenal at Harper's Ferry, located in a part of Virginia that is now West Virginia. We mentioned earlier that Brown believed he was intended to free the slaves. Since his exploits in Kansas he had, he said, "devoted his whole being, mental, moral, and physical, all that he had and was to the extinction of slavery." He had read about slave uprisings such as occurred in Haiti in the 1790s, and his plan now was revolution. Arming his men with weapons from the arsenal, he would establish a base in the Appalachian Mountains from which he would extend his warfare against the slaveholders. Then, he was sure, those in bondage "would immediately rise all over the Southern states." He had a constitution for the new state he planned to create and plans for schools where the slaves "were to be taught the useful and mechanical arts and to be instructed in all the businesses of life."

Brown's poorly conceived plans were known to a few abolitionists who sincerely believed that revolutionary tactics were necessary to free the blacks. These supporters gave him some financial assistance, but it was very small, and the manpower at his command was also very small. When he attacked Harper's Ferry in 1859, he had only 21 recruits, 16 whites and five Negroes. Within 36 hours, the arsenal had been regained under Brevet Colonel Robert E. Lee, who was ordered to Harper's Ferry by President Buchanan. Lieutenant J.E.B. Stuart played an important role in the capture. The raid claimed a total of 17 lives from both sides, and Brown's scheme proved a tragic failure in that the slaves showed no inclination to join him. Two of Brown's sons died in the debacle. Brown himself was tried by the state of Virginia and found guilty of rebellion, treason, and murder. He and four of his followers were hanged.

The South was now seized with new fear about a general slave uprising encouraged by the abolitionists. Although few Northerners condoned such a course, John Brown became the martyred hero of millions.

The people of Harriet's era were not occupied exclusively with the slavery issue, important as it was. New discoveries and inventions in science and technology were making rapid and significant changes in their lives. Samuel F.B. Morse, a painter, was the inventor of the electromagnetic telegraph. In 1844 the first message was sent over an experimental telegraph line from Washington to Baltimore. By 1850 there were thousands of telegraph lines east of the Mississippi; eight years later a transatlantic cable was laid. This was followed by transcontinental telegraph lines. The telegraph soon became associated with the railroad. Its effect was widespread—even newspapers benefited because reporters could get down the details of an event in Isaac Pitman's shorthand and then send the transcribed story over the wire. The McCormick reaper was patented in 1834, and by the eve of the Civil War 20,000 a year were being turned out. The sewing machine also has an interesting history; in the 1830s an

I have, may it please the court, a few words to say. In the first place, I deny everything but what I have all along admitted — the design on my part to free the slaves.... I never did intend murder, or treason, or the destruction of property, or to excite or incite slaves to rebellion, or to make insurrection.... It is unjust that I should suffer such a penalty. Had I interfered in the manner which I admit, and which I admit has been fairly proved ... had I so interfered in behalf of the rich, the powerful, the intelligent, the so-called great, or in behalf of any of their friends ... and suffered and sacrificed what I have in this interference, it would have been all right; and every man in this court would have deemed it an act worthy of reward rather than punishment.

This court acknowledges, as I suppose, the validity of the law of God. I see a book kissed here which I suppose to be the Bible, or at least the New Testament. That teaches me that all things whatsoever I would that men should do to me, I should do even so to them. It teaches me, further, to "remember them that are in bonds, as bound with them." I endeavored to act up to that instruction. I say, I am yet too young to understand that God is any respecter of persons. I believe that to have interfered I have done — in behalf of His despised poor, was not wrong, but right. Now it is deemed necessary that I should forfeit my life for the furtherance of the ends of justice, and mingle my blood further with the blood of my children and with the blood of millions in this slave country whose rights are disregarded by wicked, cruel, and unjust enactments — I submit; so let it be done! — *John Brown, November 2, 1859.*

American Quaker named Walter Hunt developed the idea of an eye-pointed needle and lockstitch, but he never marketed his invention because he did not want seamstresses to lose their jobs. In 1846 Elias Howe obtained a patent for a lockstitch machine and a horizontal eye-pointed needle. Within five years Isaac Singer had perfected a device with a vertical needle and a foot treadle. Singer's partner, Edward Clark, promoted the use of the new invention by selling service contracts and allowing installment buying. Thus women were now encouraged to operate mechanical devices both at home and in the factory. As the output of clothing increased, the price dropped. During the Civil War the uniforms of the Union Army were machine made — a tremendous improvement over the Confederate method of hand production. Other major American inventions of the era include the Colt pistol with its revolving cylinder and Charles Goodyear's discovery in 1836 that crude rubber could be made more durable by a process known as vulcanization.

The everyday life of the people was also improved by many inventions and discoveries of lesser importance. Some of these include the safety pin (1832 by Walter Hunt of sewing-machine fame); the balloon-frame house (1833); the white-phosphorus match (1836); the tin can (1839, but the canning industry did not develop until later); the ice box (1840); the Mason jar (1858). The first hot-air furnace was invented in 1820, but central heating developed very slowly. (Coal became a source of power after 1840. This had great industrial consequence, but it was some time before coal was used for fuel in homes.) Wood-burning cook stoves were common by mid-nineteenth century. There were few bathrooms before 1860; so the outhouse was generally used. Bathtubs existed, but in Boston as late as 1845 a doctor's prescription was considered necessary for tub bathing. Even in 1880, five out of six city inhabitants used public baths.

The technological development of the United States is mirrored today in various exhibits in the Smithsonian Institution. This great museum grew from a bequest of 100,000 pounds sterling from a British amateur scientist, James Smithson. John Quincy Adams, whom we have mentioned before, was very interested in this "establishment for the increase and diffusion of knowledge among men," and he expended much effort on its behalf.

Some cities — for example, Chicago and San Francisco — grew very rapidly. The older ones, such as Philadelphia, New York, and Boston, grew more gradually, but they all faced difficulties. In New York City, for instance, the disposal of garbage and offal presented problems by the 1830s, and even pigs roamed the unpaved streets. As crime and violence became rampant in the cities, a professional police force was needed.

The 1840s saw the arrival of huge numbers of immigrants from Europe, especially from Germany and from Ireland after 1847, the year of the devastating potato famine in that country. Of course not all the newcomers settled in New York City, but a great many did, further straining resources. Considering the conditions under which northern factory workers existed (12-hour work days, starvation wages, and appalling environments), it is not surprising that the South claimed its slaves were better off than the North's working poor. Nevertheless, the leading port of the nation had much to boast about. As early as the 1830s, there were horse-drawn omnibuses in which a passenger might ride for two or three cents, and the streets were lit with gas lamps. (Whale oil lamps were replacing candles in homes.) By 1850 hand-pumper fire engines with leather hoses were available. John Hope Franklin's fascinating *A Southern Odyssey* recounts reactions of plantation owners to northern institutions as they visited an industrial area.

Until it was established that specific microorganisms caused specific disorders, no substantial progress against infectious disease could be made. Thus tuberculosis, cholera, malaria, yellow fever, and other infectious diseases took terrific tolls. Spitting in public places was common and, ironically, far more dangerous than today because of the prevalence of tuberculosis in the population. The housewife was plagued with houseflies, as window screens were still a novelty late in the century. She was also faced with food spoilage and how to dispose of refuse. Streams and alleys reeked of decaying garbage and excrement, demonstrating a lack of sanitation.

Scientific nutrition would come later. People ate very quickly and consumed far too much. The usual diet was high in meat, and there were no salads. The availability of fruits and vegetables depended chiefly on what was in season. Many city dwellers refused to drink water, fearing cholera. Milk sometimes had "additives" such as chalk or plaster of Paris. (By 1856 Massachusetts, for example, enacted milk-reform laws.) When teeth decayed, they were extracted; so undoubtedly people of all ages had trouble chewing. Cookbooks had recipes for such items as cough medicine, rat-trap bait, and indelible ink.

With medical knowledge so limited (for example, cholera was believed by some to be a retribution for sin), quackery flourished. Until about mid-century, hydrotherapy, or water cure (used by both Harriet and Calvin), blood-letting, and the administration of emetics and purgatives were in vogue. Nostrums of all sorts were advertised in the newspapers. One of the most popular was Hosteller's Bitters, perhaps because it contained 32 percent alcohol. Related to quackery was the interest in spiritualism. (Harriet indulged in this after her oldest son drowned in 1857.) Henry Ward Beecher was very interested in phrenology, the study of the surface of the skull as indicative of mental faculties and character traits. Prospective spouses were occasionally asked to take phrenologic tests, and there was even advice in rhyme:

Know well thy skull, and note its hilly lumps:
The proper study of mankind is bumps.

As a relief to all this, we note one outstanding medical advance — the discovery in the 1840s of ether as a general anaesthetic.

The prairie settler or the gold prospector had little time for leisure. For a long time relaxation was viewed askance in the East, but gradually recreation became acceptable. Some men tried foot racing, boxing, gymnastics, wrestling, and weight lifting. The first baseball game was played in 1839. Dancing was popular in some regions; in 1842 the polka became fashionable. There was much prejudice against the theater, but during the 1840s this began to weaken. Harriet did not approve of the stage, but dramatizations of *Uncle Tom* did much to spur acceptance of theatrical productions. Theaters were in general dirty, vermin-infected firetraps, hot in summer and cold in winter, with uncomfortable seats and poor lighting. Other amusements included cock fights and horse races, as well as puppet shows and magic and minstrel shows. Some of these shows were provided by itinerant performers. The river showboat was also gaining in popularity. Riding and hunting were particularly liked in the South. (Interestingly, Catherine Beecher, as early as the 1820s, arranged for girls in her school to ride.) When the climate permitted, sleighing and skating were popular. Amelia Bloomer at mid-century advocated a costume of full trousers with a short skirt for women. This would have facilitated participation in sports, but such dress became associated with feminism. Bathing suits were not invented until after the Civil War, but "promiscuous" bathing took place in resorts such as Newport, Rhode Island, and Cape May, New Jersey. The rich also frequented such spas as Saratoga, New York, and White Sulfur Springs, Virginia.

The lyceum movement, begun in 1826, was a powerful force in the instruction of adults. Named for the place where Aristotle taught in Athens, lyceums featured noted speakers such as Henry David Thoreau, Daniel Webster, Henry Ward Beecher, Nathaniel Hawthorne, and Susan B. Anthony to inform the public about the arts, science, history, and public affairs. As a matter of fact, some of Ralph Waldo Emerson's essays were originally lyceum lectures. The lyceum movement, in its early years, stimulated great interest in establishing a public school system.

Education varied in different parts of the country. Literacy was generally low, especially in the South where public schools were not encouraged. The older northern states had public schools, with most students completing only the first eight grades, but parents who could afford to do so usually sent their offspring to private schools. Twelve reports on the Boston schools between 1837–1848 by the educator Horace Mann (known today as "the father of the common schools"), showed that the pedagogy of the day emphasized rote memory except in mathematics. The curriculum consisted of the three R's with a smattering of grammar, history, and geography; strict discipline was enforced and floggings averaged 65 per day for 400 children. In addition, teachers were poorly trained and inexperienced; pupil attendance was irregular because many parents made their children work; and buildings were generally inadequate and poorly heated. Boston, by the way, had one of the most progressive systems of all the states. Mann firmly believed in "the absolute right to an education of every human being...." His reports brought to light many deficiencies, and he was especially distressed about corporal punishment. He was successful in fighting for improvements and increased appropriations for public schools. He established free training schools for teachers (the nation's first opened in Lexington, Massachusetts, in 1839), increased the pay scale for teachers, encouraged the employment of women teachers, enlarged the curriculum, and instituted other reforms and innovations. Though his work was done while serving as secretary of the Massachusetts State Board of Education, it became known and accepted nationally. Mann succeeded John Quincy Adams in Congress where he fought for the abolition of slavery.

William McGuffey's *Eclectic Readers*—filled with virtuous sentiments—were first published in the 1830s and studied by three generations. There was also a wealth of literature aimed at children and adolescents. These magazines and books imparted moral values and exuded pride in America.

Nationalistic pride was reflected in much of the nation's culture: The books of Alexander Hamilton and LaFayette were popular, as were portraits of famous Americans and historical scenes such as Washington's *Passage of the Delaware* by Thomas Scully (1780–1872). Currier and Ives prints were always in evidence, and about a third of New England homes possessed Volume I of George Bancroft's *A History of the United States*. There were many excellent "home grown" products. James Audubon's *Birds of America* is considered today one of the great achievements of American intellectual history. The founding of the New York Philharmonic Orchestra in 1842 was a cultural landmark. *The Scarlet Letter* appeared in 1850, *Moby Dick* in 1851, and *Walden* in 1853. Other American cultural productions of the time include paintings of the North American Indians by George Catlin (1796–1872); Stephen Foster's *Old Folks at Home* (1851) and other songs; and Lowell Mason's music for *Nearer My God to Thee* (1856) and other hymns. Construction of the Washington Monument began in 1848 and continued for the next 35 years.

Although *Home Sweet Home* (words by John Howard Payne, 1792–1852) was sung by many Americans, home had different meanings for different people. The home of the Indian, for instance, was now seldom secure as the white man occupied more and more Indian land, diminished buffalo herds, and demoralized the proud race with firearms, whiskey, syphilis, and tuberculosis. It was not uncommon for a couple and their children to live in a boardinghouse or hotel. By 1840 Gothic houses were being built by those who could afford them. Papered walls were in style and heavy drapes reduced interior light. Open fireplaces had ash chutes to the cellar. All this, of course, was a far cry from the homesteader's farmhouse and the slave's hut. Many homes that could not possess a piano settled for the cheaper melodeon, or reed organ. The average farmhouse owned a dictionary, *Pilgrim's Progress*, an almanac, and perhaps a Shakespeare or a novel or so by Scott or Cooper and, of course, the Bible.

We have emphasized the role of religion in the life of the people. It did not always cause harmony, as exemplified by the dissention among the clergy over the slavery issue. There was much intolerance among Christians, as illustrated by the treatment given Catholics. An anti-Catholic mob in 1834 burned down the Ursaline Convent in Boston and drove out the nuns and their pupils; two lives were lost. Yet the only person convicted received a pardon from the governor. By 1840 about five and one half percent of the population was Roman Catholic. This almost doubled during the next 20 years, chiefly due to immigration, and there was fear that aliens would take jobs from Americans. But there was specific religious prejudice also. Indeed, the 1856 national platform of one political party included an anti-Catholic plank. (The Catholics, in turn, hated Negroes and feared competition from them.)

With life so tenuous, due largely to inadequate medical knowledge, people exhibited a providential attitude. A 16-year-old
Vermont youth wrote this in 1848:

> This life is not much. We are here but a short time & then we are called
> away. We see the great men of our nation one by one fall away & soon all
> this sett of inhabitants will be changed for a new sett.

(The writer, Merrill Ober, died when he was 21.) We recall that when
it was suggested to Harriet that she write something to condemn
slavery, she said she would *if she lived*. Letters written in the
nineteenth century show intense interest in the details of dying. This
is exemplified in a 1849 letter to a father on the death of his son from
cholera. The writer states, "I shall now give you the full particulars of
the sickness and death of George." Here is an excerpt from another
long description of a death. The letter was written in 1853:

> I sang "Majestic sweetness sits enthroned" and "All is well". J. read passages
> from the New Testament. His children were referred to; but, too overcome
> to bear more then, he said, "Let the dear children come tomorrow," evi-
> dently not thinking his hour so near. He said to us who were about him,
> "Cover me up warm, keep my utterance clear." He afterwards added, "I'm
> doing well,: — and, in a few moments, with but slight indication of the
> transition, his spirit passed away.

It was during this period that cemeteries such as Mount Auburn
in Massachusetts and Greenwood in New York became famous.

The publication of *The Origin of the Species* in 1859 had
tremendous influence on religious thinking. Some clergymen, like
Henry Ward Beecher, embraced the theory of evolution and found it
compatible with their views on the relationship between God and
man. Many vehemently rejected Darwinism, and the controversy
still rages.

False modesty flourished in Harriet's era. The topic of pregnancy
was avoided in conversation as much as possible, and it was
considered more polite to use the word "limb" rather than "leg." The
Cincinnati clergy demonstrated how absurd this sort of thing could
become: When Hiram Powers in 1843 produced a white marble
statue of a nude girl chained after her capture by the Turks (*The
Greek Slave*), they demanded an inquiry as to whether a live model
had been used. Edward Everett, the orator-statesman who preceded

Lincoln at Gettysburg, is reported to have ordered a veil for his copy of the *Apollo Belvedere* sculpture. Many even considered it bad form to have one's name in the newspaper; however, James Gordon Bennett did much to change this attitude by starting a special page in the *New York Herald* for society events.

As in every age, there were various experimental communities based on cooperative living. One of the most famous was Brook Farm in Massachusetts. Many of its members belonged to the literary and philosophical movement known as transcendentalism. New Harmony, Indiana, is remembered for establishing early a kindergarten, a free public school, a free library, and a school offering equal education to boys and girls. Most of these model communities were short-lived. Many rejected marriage, and this, like Mormon plural marriages, offended the majority of God-fearing Christians. On the other hand, it was group action that helped to conquer the prairie, where it was traditional for neighbors to help one another build structures and cultivate fields. In the cities, however, labor unions lacked organization and remained weak.

By the 1830s the word "socialism" was in use, but the idea of a welfare state was unknown. There was, however, some private philanthropy. Although *The Communist Manifesto* had come out in 1848, its influence on the United States was in the future. All manner of reforms were needed — in the treatment of prisoners, of the handicapped, and of the insane; adequate and safe water supplies were required; excessive drinking, especially in the South, was a serious problem; labor was often exploited. In time there were some improvements, but the greatest evil of all remained, and differences between North and South were not resolved. According to Senator Seward (1858), "an irrepressible conflict" would exist until the United States became either all slave or all free. The conflict was not resolved until Appomattox.

The Emancipation Proclamation had given freedom to slaves in areas not under control of the federal government. This excluded the Union border slave states of Delaware, Maryland, Missouri, and Kentucky. The Thirteenth Amendment, passed in 1865, provided:

> Neither slavery nor involuntary servitude, except as a punishment for crime whereof the party shall have been duly convicted, shall exist within the United States, or any place subject to its jurisdiction.
>
> Congress shall have power to enforce this article by appropriate legislation.

Because the Negro's quest for equality has lasted so long, the true importance of the Thirteenth Amendment may be minimized today. Nevertheless, it remains a major step toward justice for the black man in the United States.

7

Before and After Slavery

...thank God for one thing, I have lived to see slavery abolished....
— *Harriet Beecher Stowe, in a letter July 22, 1875*

Uncle Tom's Cabin, like most fiction, is strongly related to the life experience of its author; thus we are presenting in this chapter some biographical information about Harriet Beecher Stowe. The best sources of such information appear to be *The Life-Work of the Author of Uncle Tom's Cabin* by Florine Thayer McCray (1889) and *Crusader in Crinoline*, written in 1946 by Forrest Wilson. Approved biographies of her son Charles (1889) and by her friend Annie Fields (1897) may be too selective and possibly biased. But aside from that, the author herself caused confusion with differing accounts about the sources she used for *Uncle Tom*. (This may have been unimportant to her, since she maintained that God wrote *Uncle Tom's Cabin*, using her as His agent.) Then there is this comment from the Stowe-Day Foundation: "Mrs. Stowe was not meticulous in the dating of her letters nor was she consistent in providing the location of their composition." And in the preface to *Crusader in Crinoline*, Wilson states: "In any display of her personal affairs, Harriet was seldom frank ... she modified dull truth to make a good story." Despite these hindrances, there is an abundance of reliable material that covers the important aspects of her life.

The year was 1811 and the place Litchfield, Connecticut. James Madison was president but John Adams and Thomas Jefferson were still alive. Just eight years before, the young nation had doubled its size through the Louisiana Purchase. Connecticut had few Negroes, but slavery would not be abolished completely by that state until 1848. On June 14, the Reverend Lyman Beecher and his wife

Roxanna became the parents of their sixth living child. They called her Harriet Elizabeth, Harriet being the name given to another child born to them three years before who had not survived.

Lyman Beecher was minister of the Congregational Meeting in Litchfield and Connecticut's leading clergyman. Congregationalism, also called Presbyterianism, was the authorized religion of that state until 1817. It was tax supported and the keeping of the Sabbath was enforced; there was no tolerance of differing religious views. The Beechers had been in America almost as long as the Pilgrims. Lyman's father, grandfather, and great grandfather had been blacksmiths, but Lyman had the benefit of a Yale education. A man of strong emotions and puritanical beliefs, he was a perennial foe of alcohol, dueling, Catholicism, and Unitarianism. He was opposed to novels at the time of Harriet's birth, but he read widely. He was a good hunter and fisherman and also fond of music. Although a stern disciplinarian, he was nevertheless loved by his children. At an early age, they learned from him the art of logical argument, for which his sermons were famous. (He conducted three services every Sunday.) Harriet's words bear this out: "...he never seemed to realize that people were unbelievers for any other reason than want of light, and that clear and able arguments would at once put an end to skepticism."

Religion was the keynote of Lyman Beecher's life. While it imposed harsh demands, it also taught that all men were children of God. This religion was dominant and pervasive in the Beecher home. In time it would spur Lyman's seven sons to enter the ministry; in time it would spur Harriet Elizabeth to write one of the most influential books ever published.

Roxanna was the daughter of Eli Foote, a lawyer who had remained loyal to the Crown during the Revolutionary War. She had a somewhat liberal upbringing and was considered well educated. Originally a member of the Anglican faith, she later joined her husband's flock for the Episcopalian doctrine was heresy to Lyman. Roxanna probably had little direct influence on Harriet, for she died of tuberculosis when the child was only five. But there appears to have been a concerted family effort to keep her memory alive.

The village of Litchfield was settled and incorporated in 1719; it is believed to be the birthplace of Ethan Allen, leader of the Green Mountain Boys. During the Revolution, American soldiers used it as a supply point and rest stop. In 1784 Judge Tapping Reeve had estab-

lished there the country's first law school. Miss Pierce's Female Academy was located nearby, and the two institutions contributed much to the culture and prosperity of the village. Neither had dormitories, so many families boarded students. About Litchfield Harriet would write: "My earliest recollections are those of its beautiful scenery." Her brother Henry Ward regarded it as a blessed place to spend one's childhood.

The household she entered was not small. The eldest child was Catherine, also called Kate, born in 1800. It was she who would guide and supervise the motherless Harriet, or Hattie, who was 11 years her junior. Next came William, who would have pastorates in Ohio and Massachusetts. Edward, born in 1803, would earn a Phi Beta Kappa key and later become very active in the abolitionist movement. Mary, the fourth child, would marry a lawyer who became Harriet's adviser. George was born in 1807 but would die in his prime from a gunshot wound. Henry Ward, two years younger than Harriet, would become a leader in the antislavery movement as well as the greatest preacher of his era. Roxanna's last child was Charles, in 1815. He too would be antislavery, and from a true account by him the future authoress would create Simon Legree.

Several other persons lived with the Beechers: Roxanna's sister Mary Hubbard, an orphaned ward of Lyman's, two boarders from Miss Pierce's school, and two Negro bondservants. Their ramshackle dwelling was owned by Lyman, not the church, and when the family could stand no more overcrowding, Roxanna spent a small inheritance for an addition. Close by lived Lyman's stepmother and her spinster daughter Esther, who resembled Miss Ophelia.

Although her Aunt Mary died of tuberculosis just after Harriet was two, Mary's story would be retold many times as Harriet was growing up, and its significance was not lost on her. When Mary was 18, she married John Hubbard, a Jamaican planter. The bride arrived at her new home to find several mulatto children whose father, by his own admission, was her husband. In less than a year she was back in Connecticut, and the family knew that she could never tolerate his attitude that slave women should be bred like cattle.

Opposite: The Beecher family photographed by Mathew Brady, ca. 1859. Back row: Thomas K., William, Edward, Charles, Henry Ward; front row: Mrs. Hooker, Catherine, Lyman, Mrs. Perkins, Harriet Beecher Stowe; insets: James, left, and George, right. Courtesy Stowe-Day Foundation, Hartford.

From earliest childhood, Harriet had a second home. It was named Nutplains and located just outside the Connecticut town of Guilford. Grandmother Foote lived there, as did Aunt Harriet and Uncle George, who were Roxanna's sister and brother. Another uncle, Samuel Foote, was a sea captain and often stayed at Nutplains when he was ashore. Captain Foote did not agree with the Reverend Beecher's narrow theology; he was a free thinker and tolerant of many religious beliefs, considering such people as Catholics and Turks just as likely as Protestants to be good and upright.

The Footes belonged to the Episcopal Church, about which the Beecher children knew very little. They were aware that the Episcopalians in their midst celebrated Christmas by decorating their church with boughs and candles and even bright stars. But their father's church did not observe December 25, and Litchfield's merchants conducted business as usual on that day. (The Fourth of July, however, was an important holiday, especially since many of the town's men had fought in the War of Independence.)

In 1817 the beautiful Harriet Porter of Portland, Maine, became the second Mrs. Beecher. Miss Porter had noted that to succeed Roxanna was "a momentous concern." There is suspicion, but no proof, that Roxanna's children never regarded her as a substitute for their departed mother. According to Harriet, her stepmother was "naturally hard, correct, exact, and exacting." Before she died in 1835, Harriet Porter Beecher produced four children: Frederick, who died in infancy of scarlet fever; Isabella, born in 1822, who would become a leader in the fight for women's rights; Thomas K., born two years later and destined to be Elmira's (New York) beloved pastor; and James, who arrived in 1828 and would later lead a regiment of blacks and also serve as its chaplain.

A letter written by the second Mrs. Beecher mentioned that at the age of six and a half, Harriet could read well and had memorized 27 hymns and two long chapters from the Bible. (In contrast, Henry Ward, with whom Harriet would always have great empathy, was an indifferent learner whom she often tried to help.) A little later Harriet was reading *Arabian Nights*, which she had found among tracts with such titles as *An Appeal on the Unlawfulness of a Man's Marrying His Wife's Sister*. Another book intrigued the child who later became an avid reader: Cotton Mather's *Magnalia Christi Americana*, written in 1702 about Indians, witches, and sinners in Massachusetts.

By 1820 Harriet was enrolled in Miss Pierce's school. Her father, now Dr. Beecher thanks to a D.D. from a Vermont college, taught Saturday Bible classes for Miss Pierce and thus received free tuition for his children. Harriet's early education was intimately concerned with religion. To illustrate, an essay by her was read at festivities ending the school year 1823–24; its mystifying title was *Can the Immortality of the Soul Be Proved by the Light of Nature?*

Catherine took a teaching position in 1821 at a school for girls in New London, Connecticut. Very soon she became engaged to Alexander Fisher, a young professor at Yale. Before the marriage took place, however, the university sent him to Europe on business. The ship was wrecked off Ireland, and Fisher was lost. This tragedy was deepened by the fact that the young man was unconverted.

The faith embraced by Lyman Beecher held that men were born totally depraved and could attain virtue and salvation only through God's grace. There was no evidence that Fisher had undergone the personal religious experience that could put him in a state of grace, and Dr. Beecher feared Professor Fisher might never enter the Kingdom of Heaven.

Such a thought naturally caused Catherine great agony, but she was intelligent and began to reason that perhaps God would grant forgiveness to Fisher, a good man, not a depraved one as she was supposed to believe. She was the first to doubt the teachings of her father's church; other Beechers would too. For example, Henry Ward's fame as a preacher was in part due to his message about a God of love and compassion — a God who "loves a man in his sins for the sake of helping him out of them," and Harriet ultimately believed in a God of love rather than the Puritans' God of wrath. Her own so-called conversion took place when she was around 13.

The young Yale professor had left his bride-to-be his personal library, which came to be enjoyed by the Beechers. Lyman even went so far as to recommend *Ivanhoe* after he had read it. Harriet no doubt took his advice because she became a life-long admirer of the works of Sir Walter Scott. Previously she had also read *The Corsair* by Lord Byron. Aunt Esther, who loved books and had broad interests, had suggested it, much to Harriet's delight. After that, she read anything of Byron's she could find. George Gordon Noel Byron was a romantic figure, noted for his good looks and flamboyant life-style as well as his poetry. It was known that he was separated from his wife, had other women, and certainly was not a true believer, although he had had a Calvinistic upbringing. Such a person Dr.

Beecher would certainly have tried to convert; nevertheless, he recognized the genius of Byron's poetry and did not forbid his daughter to read it. Harriet found the poetry so divine that she was disinclined to believe that its author could have any serious faults. Lord Byron died in 1824, but years later, Harriet would view his character in a very different light.

The "odd little girl," as Mrs. Stowe referred to herself, left Litchfield when she was 13. Catherine had received a legacy of $2,000, and with it started a school for girls in Hartford, 30 miles from Litchfield. Mary was teaching at her sister's school and in 1824 Harriet enrolled there.

Hartford, with its population numbering several thousand, was truly a source of wonderment to Harriet. The main street was cobbled, there were stage connections with Boston and New York, and Hartford had daily newspapers and even special stores very different from Litchfield's familiar general store. She boarded with a family who had a daughter living with the Beechers while attending Miss Pierce's school, and to Harriet's special joy she was given a room of her own.

The new school had 25 pupils that year and the tuition was $6 a quarter. Although Harriet was shy, she soon became friendly with a Hartford girl named Georgiana May. This would be a lifelong friendship, and Harriet's third daughter was named Georgiana May Stowe. It was clear that Harriet was a rapid learner with an exceptional memory. Catherine planned to use her as a teacher and soon put her in charge of a class studying *The Analogy of Religion, Natural and Revealed, to the Constitution and Course of Nature*, a book written by an English moral philosopher and theologian. Otherwise, Harriet was a student. To Grandmother Foote she wrote, "I devote most of my time to Latin and arithmetic." Later, when she was a regular faculty member, she taught rhetoric and composition. Meanwhile, her sister's school was expanding rapidly and gaining reputation in educational circles.

The year 1826 brought upheaval to the Beecher family. Dr. Beecher, now 50 and very prominent in ecclesiastical circles, accepted a call to the Hanover Street Church in Boston. Grandmother Beecher was dead, and Aunt Esther had been living with Lyman's family. Not enthusiastic about moving to a new parsonage, Esther compromised by going first to Hartford for a year to keep house for her three teacher-nieces. At about the same time, Edward, graduated from Yale and Andover Theological Seminary, was called to the pastorate of Boston's Park Street Church. So Lyman had an added reinforcement for his fight against rum, gambling, and Unitarianism.

At 15 Harriet was quiet and introspective, occupied with the sin she thought was within her. Even a visit to Nutplains, accompanied by Georgianna, did not lessen her depression. Such worry may be difficult for today's reader to understand, but the reader was not reared in the faith of the Puritans; nor does he live in an era when religion was a national concern. As mentioned, Harriet gradually worked out her spiritual problems, finding repose in the love of Jesus Christ. Her faith is expressed in a hymn she wrote later:

Still, Still with Thee

Still, still with Thee, when purple morning breaketh,
  When the bird waketh and the shadows flee;
Fairer than morning, lovlier than the daylight,
  Dawns the sweet consciousness, *I am with Thee!*

Alone with Thee! amid the mystic shadows,
  The solemn hush of nature newly born;
Alone with Thee in breathless adoration,
  In the calm dew and freshness of the morn.

As in the dawning, o'er the waveless ocean,
  The image of the morning star doth rest,
So, in this stillness, Thou beholdest only
  Thine image in the waters of my breast.

Still, still with Thee! As to each new-born morning
  A fresh and solemn splendor still is given,
So doth this blessed consciousness, awaking,
  Breathe each new day nearness to Thee and heaven.

When sinks the soul, subdued by toil, to slumber,
  Its closing eye looks up to Thee in prayer,
Sweet the repose beneath Thy wings o'ershading,
  But sweeter still to wake and find Thee there.

So shall it be at last, in that bright morning,
  When the soul waketh, and life's shadows flee;
Oh! in that hour, fairer than daylight dawning,
  Shall rise the glorious thought — *I am with Thee.*

— from *A Treasure of Hymns*
by Amos R. Wells, 1914

This faith would play a major role in her destiny. At 17 she wrote prophetically to Edward: "I do not mean to live in vain. He has given me talents, And I will lay them at His feet...."

By 1828 Harriet was a young lady. How did she look? Daguerreotype portraits were not available at that time, but she is described as being very small, with a broad forehead, blue-violet eyes, an aquiline nose, a generous mouth, and brown hair worn in curls. She was given to spells of reverie which did not enhance her physical attractiveness. But when she was paying close attention to her surroundings, she was animated and interesting. A keen sense of humor was another plus. So far there had been no young man in her life.

Perhaps Dr. Beecher found the fight against Unitarianism in Boston too uphill for his liking. At any rate, he was soon setting his sights on Cincinnati. In 1830 he wrote to Catherine that "the moral destiny of our nation, and all its institutions and hopes, and the world's hopes, turns on the character of the West, and the competition now is for that of preoccupancy in the education of the rising generation, in which Catholics and infidels have got the start on us." In 1832 he accepted the presidency of Cincinnati's new theological seminary and the pastorate of its Second Presbyterian Church.

Again the Beechers faced a major move. As many as could were to assume the challenge, leaving the East whenever possible. Edward was already in the West, serving as president of Illinois College at Jacksonville. Samuel Foote, now married and no longer at sea, was making Cincinnati his home. Catherine had turned over her school, which now enrolled more than 100 students, to a very able male educator; so she was free to found a similar western institution, and it was assumed that Harriet would teach at it. George would enroll at the new Lane Seminary. The trek therefore would include Dr. and Mrs. Beecher, Aunt Esther, Catherine, Harriet, George, Isabella, Thomas, and little James, all traveling together. Others would reach Ohio later, for William was preaching in Ohio, Henry Ward was attending Amherst College, and Charles was a student at Bowdoin in Maine. Mary was married and living in Hartford, so she would not be a part of her father's latest proselyting effort.

The Beechers' westward migration began in October, 1832, with New York the first stopping point. There and wherever else possible, they stayed with friends rather than paying for accommodations. Lane Seminary was in need of an endowment for the professorship of biblical literature, and Lyman managed to solicit some generous donations while visiting the metropolis. Then it was on to Philadelphia by stagecoach. The journey appears to have been something of a crusade; by Harriet's account, George and the children distributed tracts to wayfarers, and she mentioned "peppering the land with moral influence." They were in Harrisburg on a Sunday, and of course arrangements were made for the father of the clan to preach. Next came the Alleghanies, and Lyman hired a coach and horses rather than using a stage again.

Harriet had traveled little during her life, but her writings on the journey do not give her thoughts on the magnificant natural panorama that she must have witnessed. One letter did, however, mention something of significance about the professorship of biblical literature: "The incumbent is to be C. Stowe." A few years before, Calvin Stowe had worked with her father in Boston, and Harriet knew him by sight.

Avoiding the stage proved to be a poor move for the Beecher contingent; the hired horses took eight days to get them to Wheeling, which is now in West Virginia. There disconcerting news awaited them: A cholera epidemic was raging in Cincinnati. The caravan halted temporarily on the east bank of the Ohio until it was deemed safe to live in their new home. The delay of two weeks was put to good use — the eminent Dr. Beecher preached 11 times in Wheeling.

At last the Ohio River was crossed. They were again in a stage, their missionary zeal unimpaired. There was singing and tract distribution, plus jouncing and bumping as the wheels encountered log-paved roads. (Almost 20 years later, Harriet would describe a wild ride over an Ohio corduroy road with Cudjoe and Senator Bird attempting to get Eliza and little Harry to safety.) On they went, by way of Columbus, and arrived in Cincinnati on November 14.

Cincinnati represented the industry of the growing nation. In 1811 the first steamboat in western waters arrived there from Pittsburgh, going downstream. As noted previously, the South was reluctant to manufacture necessities, and because Cincinnati was a riverport, it grew rapidly as a supply center for the area south of it. Then in 1832 the Miami and Erie Canal was completed to Dayton, making a waterway for shipping goods eastward. Thus Cincinnati's location on the Ohio was a major factor in its prosperity in an era when commerce by water was so important. (And soon to come as an important mode of transportation was the "iron horse.")

When Harriet moved there, Cincinnati's population had reached 30,000 and consisted mainly of Easterners and German immigrants. There were meat-packing establishments, breweries, sawmills, paper mills, cotton mills, ship-building concerns, and so on. The city boasted several newspapers and even had magazine and book publishers. There were hotels and numerous churches. Education was not neglected, with free education offered to boys whose parents could not afford tuition; there were theaters and plans for a public library. In short, Cincinnati was a growing frontier town, thriving commercially and striving to have some semblance of culture.

The Beechers lived in temporary quarters until Lyman's two-story brick house was completed. Both the residence and the seminary were located in a beautiful spot called Walnut Hills, about two miles outside the city proper. Harriet busied herself writing a geography for children, begun while she was in the East. It was published in the Spring of 1833 by Cincinnati's Corey and Fairbanks. Catherine had been involved in getting the book started, and because she was known as an educator advertisements carried her name as the author. Nevertheless, Harriet was the chief author.

By May, Catherine's Western Female Institute had become a reality. To Harriet's joy, one of the teachers selected was Mary Dutton, with whom she had taught in Hartford. Catherine and Harriet took rooms together near the new school, where Harriet worked hard, with little excitement in her life. But through Mary Dutton she had one unforgettable experience.

That summer Miss Dutton was invited to visit in Kentucky, and she in turn asked Harriet to accompany her. The two New England school marms took a steamboat down the Ohio to Maysville, about 60 miles south of Cincinnati. Their host had a village home, but within a few miles of it there were large plantations that had slave quarters. Harriet's more recent biographers believe that it was on the latter she based her description of the Shelby plantation. Apparently what she saw of plantation life did not move her to comment; in fact, she dropped into one of her exasperating states of reverie. But it cannot be assumed that she was oblivious to her surroundings, for Mary Dutton would write many years later:

> Hattie did not seem to notice anything in particular that happened, but sat much of the time abstracted in thought.... Afterwards, however, in reading "Uncle Tom" I recognized scene after scene of that visit portrayed with the

most minute fidelity, and knew at once where the material for that portion of the story had been gathered.

Harriet's liberal Uncle Samuel Foote was already prominent in Cincinnati. He urged her to join a literary group, the Semi-Colon Club, which he had founded. The members met weekly, often at his home. The reader chosen for the evening presented literary contributions from the group, and these could be anonymous or otherwise. After the pieces were discussed, there was socializing and refreshments were served. The membership included persons with talents and abilities in a variety of fields, among them an astronomer, a woman novelist whose works would champion slavery, an anti-slavery leader destined to become a Chief Justice of the Supreme Court under Lincoln, and a physician-author who was responsible for naming Ohio the Buckeye State. There were also some local editors. One of the latter showed unusual interest in a New England sketch read at a meeting of the group. The author was Harriet, who had preferred to submit it without her name. This editor's approval led her to expand and improve the story she had written. It was published in his *Western Monthly Magazine* in April, 1834. It not only won her $50, but it made her realize her potential as a writer. This success had another significance: It impressed her family so much that from then on, they considered their Hattie an authoress. Such approbation no doubt reinforced the self-esteem of the young woman who had dwelled so long in the shadow of her father and sister. So the Semi-Colon Club was a bright spot in Harriet's life.

When Calvin Stowe arrived in Cincinnati, his bride Eliza Tyler accompanied him. In a short time, Harriet and the attractive Mrs. Stowe were close friends. They had somewhat similar backgrounds — Eliza's father was also a Presbyterian minister — and they were roughly the same age. Eliza and her husband were members of the Semi-Colon Club, and this is noteworthy because Calvin's early impression of Harriet must have associated her with writing.

In June of 1834 Harriet returned to New England for Henry Ward's graduation from Amherst College in Massachusetts. She managed to visit Georgiana May and also stayed with her grandmother in Nutplains. While still in the East, she learned that her new friend Eliza Stowe was dead, presumably from tuberculosis, the scourge of the day.

It was that same summer that Lane's enrollment suffered seriously because of the withdrawal of Weld and his followers. This withdrawal would spell the ultimate end of Lyman Beecher's hope to proselyte the West and eventually he and his children would move back to the East. No doubt it was painful for Harriet to see her father defeated by a younger though able man. And the upheaval must have opened her eyes to the serious division of opinion on how to resolve the problem of slavery. We should note here that Harriet's large correspondence — and she wrote numerous and long letters — reflect little interest in political issues. But her correspondence does dwell on religious matters. To her, slavery was an evil and one that no true follower of Christ would tolerate. For this reason she was always contemptuous of the proslavery clergy. In Cincinnati the existence of slavery was all too evident.

By the fall of 1834 Henry Ward and Charles Beecher were enrolled at Lane. Catherine was traveling on behalf of higher education for women, and the running of her school was in the hands of Mary Dutton and Harriet. By now some of Harriet's stories originally published in the *Western Monthly Magazine* had been reprinted in a Cincinnati daily paper called the *Chronicle*. During the winter, the city's Presbyterian weekly, the *Journal*, carried articles by Harriet, reporting on sermons given by Professor Stowe at the Second Church.

After Eliza Stowe's death, the grieving widower turned to his wife's friend, Harriet. Stowe was Dr. Beecher's lieutenant, and it was natural that both Harriet and Calvin would be involved in various affairs pertaining to Lane and to the Second Church. And both were members of the Semi-Colon Club. As the pain of Eliza's death became less acute, a courtship began, culminating in marriage in January, 1836.

What sort of a man did Harriet marry? Her various biographers have speculated about Harriet's relationship to Calvin, but no one can speak with authority. Much is known, however, about Professor Stowe. Calvin Ellis Stowe, in common with his new wife, was a New Englander. He was born nine years before Harriet in Natick, Massachusetts. His father died when he was six, and he lived in poverty, some of the time with a grandmother. He read whatever he could lay his hands on and is said to have memorized *Pilgrim's Progress*, which he admired. By the age of 14 he was apprenticed to a paper maker who required him to start fires at the mill by 3 A.M.; so when the men came to work there would be adequate steam. Somehow the boy gained enough education to enter Bowdoin College, from which he graduated in 1824. (Franklin Pierce, later the fourteenth president, was a classmate and supposedly confessed that he got good marks in examinations by sitting next to Stowe.) By the time Calvin reached 26 years of age, he had earned a Master's degree and also a diploma from Andover Theological Seminary. Before accepting the position at Lane, he had taught at distinguished eastern establishments, including Dartmouth College. He was a scholar — in fact, the leading authority of his day of the histories of the books of the Bible. (He had a real facility for ancient languages but was also well versed in modern German.) As to his physical appearance, we know that Calvin was a stocky man but did not tend to obesity until he was past 50. At the time of his marriage to Harriet, he was clean shaven, wore sideburns, and was beginning to show a receding hairline. He would not have been considered handsome, but he presented a good appearance. The Stowe personality was engaging, and Calvin was good company. His erudition was matched by a fine sense of humor, and he was noted for his story telling. Indeed, years after she met her husband, Harriet wrote a popular book entitled *Oldtown Folks,* which depicted New Englanders in Calvin's own words. If Harriet had periods of reverie that were peculiar, Calvin's "visions" were more so. From childhood on, he experienced apparitions of various types; he saw, for instance, the devil and sometimes Indians. He could see and hear the objects of his visions, though he could not touch them. But he did have "serious doubts as to the objectivity of the scenes exhibited." Calvin was also a notorious hypochondriac.

The daughter of Lyman Beecher could be expected to hold in high regard Calvin's qualifications in the field of religion. A studious person herself, she must have appreciated his learning. And his wit must have appealed to her own sense of humor. Calvin had the approbation of Harriet's father, of course, and he was also a favorite of Henry Ward, whose preaching about the warmth of God's love brought solace to thousands. Henry attributed much of his own understanding of the Bible to Calvin Stowe's instruction.

If *Uncle Tom's* success provoked jealousy in Calvin, he did not show it. Apparently he accorded his wife the same respect she showed him. Above all, he encouraged her writing. They lived through want and uncertainty to be thrown into sudden wealth; likewise they experienced tragedy: Death took one of their sons in infancy, another during his college years, and alcoholism claimed a third who disappeared forever. But their marriage survived these ups and downs.

Although he had a new son-in-law, events had taken a bad turn for Lyman. While his second wife was dying, he had to defend himself against a charge of heresy. The latter was based on statements made in a sermon delivered by Dr. Beecher ten years earlier. (Such a charge seems today almost incomprehensible.) Old pro that he was, he came through this trial with flying colors.

Four months after his marriage to Harriet, Calvin made an extended trip to Europe, doing business for both Lane and the state of Ohio. (That state was in the process of organizing a system of public education and wanted information on European schools.) This was the first of many long separations for the couple—advantageous to Stowe historians because these separations produced many letters. When Calvin returned to the United States in 1837, he was the father of twin girls. Harriet had already named them Eliza Tyler and Isabella Beecher, but Calvin insisted that Isabella's name be changed to Harriet; so the professor's twins were named for his two wives.

While Calvin was abroad, Harriet was spending an eventful summer in Cincinnati. Much of the action centered around James Birney, who by 1836 was publishing his abolitionist paper, *The Philanthropist*, in Cincinnati. In mid-July, the paper's print shop was broken into and damaged. In late July an organized mob of anti-abolitionists became violent. These people, numbering more than 1,000 and mostly "young men of the better class," attempted to make Birney and others of the same beliefs leave town. They ordered merchants to declare themselves publicly proslavery or suffer the consequences. The violence reigned for several days, but Birney and his cohorts managed to evade the rioters. The printing press was attacked again, but the August 5 issue of the *Philanthropist* came out on time. Harriet's comment to Calvin was:

> For my part, I can easily see how such proceedings may make converts to abolitionism for already my sympathies are strongly enlisted for Mr. Birney, and I hope he will stand his ground and assert his rights. The office is fire-proof, and enclosed by high walls, I wish he would man it with armed men and see what can be done. If I were a man I would go, for one, and take good care of at least one window.

Strong feelings from a sheltered—and pregnant—school teacher!

That summer Henry Ward was temporarily editing the *Journal* with Harriet's assistance. His published views were definitely anti-slavery, though he refused to ally himself with the abolitionists. Nevertheless, the anti-Birney riots forced both Henry and Harriet to face the slavery issue as they never had before.

In common with most women of her day, Harriet's life became one of continuing childbearing; before leaving Cincinnati in 1850, the Stowes had four more children — Henry Ellis, Frederick William, Georgiana May, and Samuel Charles. (It is said that when someone complimented Calvin on his children, he replied, "Beechers, every one of them!") Harriet found great joy in her family and was a devoted mother. To Georgiana May she confided that she considered herself a fortunate woman, both in husband and children.)

The financial panic of 1837 brought hardship to many. The Western Female Institute failed, Samuel Foote went bankrupt, and Lane had only a few students — so few that Calvin Stowe knew he would leave if it were not for loyalty to Dr. Beecher. As the years went by, Lane often failed to pay his whole salary; one of Harriet's letters to Georgie mentioned that "$600 is the very most we can hope to collect of our salary, once $1200." In a family constantly short of money, the cash from Harriet's writing was most welcome, and in 1843 Harper published *The Mayflower*, a series of her New England sketches.

The Cincinnati years were particularly trying for Harriet, especially in the hot, oppressive summers. She yearned to be in New England. Instead she had to face the reality of a growing family and her husband's precarious financial situation. Domestic service was relatively cheap, and she did secure such help. But to add to her miseries, cholera was almost as likely to erupt in Cincinnati as the race riots that shook that border city from time to time. Harriet's despondency is reflected in letters to Calvin:

> If I could sew every day for a month to come, I should not be able to accomplish half of what is to be done....
>
> I am sick of the smell of sour milk, and sour meat, and sour everything, and the clothes will not dry, and no wet thing does, and everything smells moldy; and altogether I feel as if I never wanted to eat again.

When her depression became very severe, charitable friends arranged for Harriet to go to Brattleboro, Vermont, for hydrotherapy. She was gone for 15 months, leaving Calvin in charge of the children. She returned in much better health and spirits.

But now, at 45, the bleakness of Calvin's situation was beginning to affect him. Since Dr. Beecher's dream of making Lane a Yale or Andover of the West had not materialized, Calvin was concerned about his own professional future. For 15 years he had labored for Lane, with his family living hand to mouth (by 1848 there were six Stowe children). During this time, he had had no real vacation, but finally Lane granted him a leave of absence. So he, too, spent 15 months in Brattleboro. Gold was discovered in California that year, but Harriet had even less money than usual to run the household; she took in boarders and ran some sort of a school to make ends meet. She did no professional writing during this time.

In the summer of 1849 another cholera epidemic hit Cincinnati, this one so severe that a newspaper reported that it was difficult to keep up the supply of coffins needed. Superstition had it that the smoke from bituminous coal would protect people from whatever there was in the air that caused the disease; so soft coal was kept burning in all of the street corners. As a result, there was soot everywhere, outdoors and indoors. (Of course this great inconvenience was futile; cholera is caused by a microorganism and its spread in epidemics is commonly due to the fecal contamination of water supplies.) People were terrified, and many resorted to drunkenness to quell their panic. Harriet warned Calvin not to come, and she faced the ordeal with courage. Her journal entries show the dread uppermost in her mind, mentioning that any slight or minor illness "seems a death sentence." The black woman who had done the family wash one day was dead the next. Then baby Charley (Samuel Charles) was stricken. Harriet wrote to Calvin:

> At last it is over, and our little one is gone from us. He is now among the blessed.... Yet I have just seen him in his death agony, looking on his imploring face when I could not help nor soothe nor do one thing, not one, to mitigate his cruel suffering—do nothing but pray in my anguish that he might die soon. I write as though there were no sorrow like my sorrow, yet there has been in this city, as in the land of Egypt, scarce a house without its dead. This heartbreak, this anguish, has been everywhere, and when it will end God alone knows.

One year later she wrote to a friend: "I cannot open his little drawer of clothes without feeling it through my very heart." Harriet was identifying with the character Mrs. Bird when the latter opened a drawer containing her dead child's possessions, and, as she wept, selected some for Eliza's Harry. After the publication of *Uncle Tom*, a letter contained this information:

> It was at his dying bed and at his grave that I learned what a poor slave mother may feel when her child is torn away from her... I allude to this here because I have often felt that much that is in that book had its roots in the awful scenes and bitter sorrows of that summer.

Lane leased property of free blacks and from them Harriet heard much about slavery. She taught their children and often hired some of the women for household chores. One of these who particularly impressed her was called Eliza Buck. According to Harriet:

> She lived through the whole sad story of a Virginia-raised slave's life. In her youth she must have been a very handsome mulatto girl. Her voice was sweet and her manners refined and agreeable. She was raised in a good family, as nurse and sempstress. When the family became embarrassed, she was suddenly sold on to a plantation in Louisiana. She has often told me how without any warning, she was suddenly forced into a carriage, and saw her little mistress screaming and stretching her arms from the window towards her, as she was driven away. She has told me of scenes on the Louisiana plantations and how she has often been out in the night by stealth, ministering to poor slaves, who had been mangled and lacerated by the whip. Thence she was sold again into Kentucky, and her last master was the father of all her children....

Another post-*Uncle Tom* letter said:

> Again — In the scene on the boat when the woman is inveigled on board by a trader on false pretenses.
>
> I was on board that boat on the Ohio some ten years ago when a trader brought a woman on board under exactly the pretext I thus described — the scene that followed — her incredulity — her assertion that her master couldn't have cheated her so and all occurred just as I have related.... The only difference is that she had not an infant with her but a boy of eight years — but Mr. Thome I think — a gentleman whom I was acquainted with relates that he has seen an infant taken from the mothers breast and sold for a dollar at the steam boat landing when the mother was to be sold down river.

The letter also told of a three-year-old who was to be sold unless the mother could raise $200. Fortunately, "the child was redeemed by subscription in our neighborhood."

One black domestic claimed she was free, but the truth emerged: She had escaped from a Kentucky plantation, and now her owner was in Cincinnati looking for her. Harriet had the woman hidden away in a distant farmhouse belonging to an abolitionist.

These and many other incidents concerning slaves were firmly imprinted in Harriet's consciousness. They would be recalled after she left Cincinnati. She made her departure in 1850, elated to shake its dust from her feet.

As we have seen, Harriet's masterpiece was written during the Stowes' stay in Maine. Its publication in book form made Harriet for some years the most famous woman in America. She visited Lincoln at the White House to assure herself that the Emancipation Proclamation would take effect on January 1, 1863, even if the South returned to the Union. On meeting Harriet, the President is alleged to have said, "So this is the little lady who made the big war."

On the invitation of two Glasgow antislavery societies, the Stowes in 1853 visited England and Scotland with all expenses paid. Harriet's reception was phenomenal; she was not only entertained by the great, but greeted at every turn by crowds of admirers from all walks of life. Her visit prompted an "affectionate and Christian address to the women of America" beseeching them to abolish slavery. The signatures of more than 500,000 women were bound in 26 Morocco volumes and presented to her. Authorities now agree that this lionizing was not entirely due to *Uncle Tom*. The United States was less than 100 years old and on the way to becoming one of the foremost nations of the world, but it had not emancipated its slaves, and for this deserved criticism. England had abolished colonial slavery only 19 years before and continued as the chief buyer of American cotton, yet the mother country made Harriet's visit an opportunity to reprove its errant offspring. During the Civil War, when British sentiment was leaning toward the South, Harriet answered the women of England in an open letter, urging them to support the Union cause.

A Key to Uncle Tom's Cabin followed *Uncle Tom*. This was Harriet's attempt to explain the authenticity of her novel. The second work was factual, not fictional, and leaned heavily on Weld's *American Slavery As It Is*. A second antislavery novel entitled *Dred: A Tale of the Great Dismal Swamp* was published in 1856. Over the years Harriet continued to produce many magazine articles and books. Of the latter, *Oldtown Folks* (1869) and *Oldtown Fireside*

Harriet Beecher Stowe, 1811–1896. From the original painting by Chappel. Courtesy National Archives.

Stories (1872) have been acclaimed. But most critics agree that none of her succeeding books is in a class with *Uncle Tom's Cabin.*

The Stowes lived in Andover for 11 years. After Calvin's retirement they moved to Hartford, Connecticut. Their second home in that city is now the Stowe-Day Memorial Library and Historical Foundation, chartered in 1941 by the Connecticut Legislature. Harriet also purchased property in Mandarin, Florida, in 1867, and the family spent much time there.

Uncle Tom established Harriet in literary circles. In England she met writers such as Kingsley, Ruskin, and Dickens. Later she corresponded with George Eliot. In this country she became friendly with such figures as Oliver Wendell Holmes and Mark Twain.

Unfortunately, Harriet's literary reputation was damaged by *The True Story of Lady Byron's Life*, written by her and published in the *Atlantic Monthly* and in *Macmillan's Magazine* (London) in 1869. In the course of her three European visits, Harriet had become acquainted with Lady Byron. In 1856 the widow of the poet confided to Harriet that during their brief marriage her husband had been carrying on an incestuous relationship with his married half-sister. In 1868, almost ten years after Lady Byron's death, a woman who had been Byron's mistress in the 1820s published *My Recollections of Lord Byron's Life*. In it she suggested that Lady Byron's coldness had been responsible for the poet's leaving England. This infuriated Harriet, and despite warning from Calvin she rushed to the defense of her beloved, dead friend. Many Americans, as well as Britishers, were extremely critical of the article. Subscribers cancelled their subscriptions to the *Atlantic Monthly*, and the English were enraged that a foreigner dared attack their adored poet. (We must remember that this was during the Victorian Age when anything pertaining to sex was considered obscene.) A good appraisal of the affair was written by Thomas Wentworth Higginson, abolitionist and author, as part of an obituary on Harriet:

> she startled the repose of society by publishing ... what she conceived to be the true story of Lord Byron's quarrel with his wife, afterwards amplified and published (1869) as *Lady Byron Vindicated*. It was a revelation so utterly ghastly that it aroused a large part of her readers against it; and as it was incapable of further proof — resting entirely upon verbal statements of Lady Byron — it never succeeded in establishing itself in the public mind. That Mrs. Stowe fully believed her own theory as to Lord Byron is unquestionable, but the motive of the exposure still remains unexplained....

During the 1870s the Beecher-Tilton scandal caused Harriet much anguish. Henry Ward was accused of adultery involving Elizabeth Tilton, the wife of Theodore Tilton, a friend and *protégé* of Beecher's. The case came to trial in 1875; it lasted for months and was a source of numerous sensational newspaper accounts. Although the final vote of the jury was nine to three against Theodore Tilton (who was suing for adultery), few believed that Henry Ward was innocent.

About the trial, Harriet wrote to George Eliot: "This has drawn on my life — my heart's blood. He is myself; I know that you are the kind of woman to understand me when I say that I felt a blow at him more than at myself." Harriet lived until 1896, but her faculties failed during the last seven years of her life.

In 1889 author Kirk Monroe (also brother-in-law of Charles Stowe) wrote this about the author of *Uncle Tom's Cabin*:

> Not only does she stand in the foremost rank of famous women of the world, but, in shaping the destiny of the American people at a most critical period of their history, her influence was probably greater than that of any other individual. Charles Sumner said that if *Uncle Tom's Cabin* had not been written, Abraham Lincoln could not have been elected President of the United States.... Of course the abolition of slavery in America was not, and could not have been, accomplished by any one person. It was the united efforts of Mrs. Stowe with her wonderful book, of Garrison with his *Liberator*, of Whittier with his freedom-breathing poetry, of Sumner in the senate-chamber, of Wendell Phillips with his caustic wit and unanswerable arguments, of Frederick Douglass with his convincing tales of personal wrong, of Gamaliel Bailey with his *National Era*, of Theodore Weld, the abolitionist pioneer, of James Birney, and of a host of other heroic workers, besides the thousands of brave souls who cheerfully offered their lives on the battle-field; but the greatest and most far-reaching of all these influences was that of *Uncle Tom's Cabin*.

8

Retrospect

We come to recognize at work in the book, a first-rate modern social intelligence.

—*Edmund Wilson, 1948*

"We do not recollect any production of an American writer that has excited more profound and general interest. Since the commencement of the publication in our columns, we have received literally thousands of testimonials from our renewing subscribers, to its unsurpassed ability." So wrote the editor of the *National Era* in the issue containing the last installment of *Uncle Tom's Cabin*.

"It is everywhere: drawing room, nursery, kitchen, library, physician's waiting room," declared a reviewer after the story had appeared in book form. "We have nothing like it in the previous history of books."

Very soon John Jewett brought out a one-volume paperbound edition at 37 and a half cents, and at the end of one year, hard and softbound American copies in print totaled around 300,000. Some reached the slave states, of course, but generally speaking, the book was banned in the South. The population of the free states was about 13.5 million, and this number includes children, illiterates, and aliens. (With regard to the latter, special German and Welsh editions were made available.) Obviously, a great many persons were exposed to the book, considering the fact that reading aloud to several people was a common practice of the time. However, Lewis Saum, in a book that seeks to convey and analyze the writings of the era's ordinary people with regard to matters they deemed important, noted "infrequent mentions of *Uncle Tom's Cabin*."

In Britain and her colonies, more than a million and a half copies of *Uncle Tom* were circulated during the book's first year. The story was serialized daily in Paris and Stockholm; there were Italian, Spanish, Russian, Danish, Flemish, Polish, Portugese, Bohemian, Hungarian, and Armenian translations, to name only some. Of the numerous foreign publishers involved, only one paid royalties (Thomas Bosworth, who undertook to pay six cents a copy), and Harriet had no legal recourse.

Ironically, in 1854 Jewett sold out Harriet's rights and holdings to Phillips, Sampson, and Company, a publishing house that had turned her down. Eight years later Houghton Mifflin took over the rights. Currently there are more than a dozen modern American editions produced by various publishers.

Today a best-selling novel is often made into a movie, at great financial gain to its author. But *Uncle Tom's Cabin* was dramatized for the stage without recompense to Harriet — indeed, without her permission. She, as many religious persons of her day, did not approve of the theater. Very soon after *Uncle Tom* appeared in book form, a popular temperance singer named Asa Hutchinson asked permission to dramatize it. Harriet refused, saying this:

> It is thought, with the present state of theatrical performances in this county, that any attempt on the part of Christians to identify themselves with them will be productive of danger to the individual character, and to the general cause.

But even earlier, while *Uncle Tom's Cabin* was still appearing in the *National Era*, a play entitled *Uncle Tom's Cabin As It Is* opened in Baltimore on January 5, 1852. The first successful adaptation was written by George L. Aiken, an actor. This version omitted life on the Legree plantation and was first performed by the G.C. Howard Stock Company in Troy, New York, on September 27, 1852. But the public wanted the complete story, which Aikens ultimately produced. After a run in Troy, the production moved to New York City. Very soon other versions were appearing, including a production by P.T. Barnum of circus fame. Aikens complained to the *New York Atlas* about how his script had been changed by a Charles W. Taylor. The newspaper replied:

> No one is entitled to any great credit for dramatizing *Uncle Tom's Cabin*. The work of Mrs. Stowe is exceedingly dramatic from beginning to end, and anyone who will divide it into dialogue will have a perfect drama at his

hands. All who have dramatized it, have detracted from its merits by lugging in expletive characters, such as Yankees and Dutchmen. Play the book as it came from the hands of Mrs. Stowe, and it will best suit the tastes of the public.

But with more and more versions and more and more troupes to play them, the book was seldom followed. For example, in one script, Legree kills St. Clare and is in turn shot by Marks, who orders Sambo and Quimbo to "throw him to the hogs." (In the original, Legree never meets St. Clare, and the reformed Marks is last seen in Indiana.) And more and more the comic and melodramatic elements were exploited; Topsy, for instance, sang comic songs and became a caricature. A few versions were even proslavery! Nevertheless, the story of *Uncle Tom's Cabin*, despite the range of variations, remained for 80 years America's most popular play, with well-known actors such as Otis Skinner playing the part of Tom (pugilist John L. Sullivan once played Legree). As time went on, many who had not read the book saw the play and formed their opinion of the book from what they saw on the stage. Foreign stage productions abounded.

Besides the play, there were other derivatives of *Uncle Tom*, among them dolls, teaspoons, card games, cartoons, advertisements, and even wallpaper. *The Waverly Magazine* in 1853 noted:

> That immortal hero has been dramatized, painted, played, sung and danced, ... exhibited on handkerchiefs, and painted upon porcelain. There have been Uncle Tom pipes and Uncle Tom candies, Uncle Tom coats and Uncle Tom chariots. And the white characters of the book share in the general glorification.

As fiction, *Uncle Tom's Cabin* merits literary criticism. (Whittier, for one, appeared more interested in its polemic merit and overlooked it as literature.) Charles Dickens in 1852 wrote that *Uncle Tom* is "not free from the fault of over-strained conclusions and violent extremes." But he also pronounced it "a noble work, full of high power, lofty humanity, the gentlest, sweetest, and yet boldest writing." George Sand declared that the book's defects

> exist only in relation to the conventional rules of art, which have never been and never will be absolute. If its judges, possessed with the love of what they call "artistic work", find unskilled treatment in the book, look well at them to see if their eyes are dry when they are reading this or that chapter.

Other contemporary authors praised *Uncle Tom's Cabin*. Tolstoi referred to it as a model of higher art and Lowell wrote:

> the secret of Mrs. Stowe's power lay in that same genius by which the great successes in creative literature have always been achieved, — the genius that instinctively goes to the organic elements of human nature, whether under a white skin or a black, and which disregards as trivial the conventions and fictitious notions which make so large a part both of our thinking and feeling....

Reviewing the book in the *Southern Literary Messenger*, a critic who vehemently disapproved of *Uncle Tom's* purpose described its author as "possessed of a happy faculty of description, an easy and natural style, an uncommon command of pathos and considerable dramatic skill." Of Harriet, *The London Times* review said:

> The lady has great skill in the delineation of character; her hand is vigorous and firm, her mastery over human feeling is unquestionable, and her humorous efforts are unimpeachable.... But even as an artist Mrs. Stowe is not faultless. She exhibits but ordinary skill in the construction of her story. Her narrative is rather a succession of detached scenes than a compact, well-jointed whole; and many of the scenes are tedious from their similarity and repetition. The reader is interested in the fate of two heroes, but their streams of adventure never blend....

An anonymous article in *Putnam's Monthly* in 1853 declared:

> it is the consummate art of the story teller that has given popularity to *Uncle Tom's Cabin*, and nothing else. The anti-slavery sentiment obtruded by the author in her own person, upon the notice of the reader, must be felt by everyone, to be the great blemish of the book; and it is one of the proofs of its great merits as a romance, that it has succeeded in spite of this defect. If Mrs. Stowe would permit some judicious friend to run his pen through these excrescences, and to obliterate a flippant attempt at Pickwickian humor, here and there, *Uncle Tom's Cabin* would be a nearly perfect work of art, and would deserve to be placed by the side of the greatest romances the world has known.

After the Civil War, John William DeForest pronounced *Uncle Tom* "a picture of American Life, drawn with a few strong and passionate strokes, not filled in thoroughly, but still a portrait."

In 1893, a Southerner wrote in the *Sewanee Review*:

> The truth is that if there had not been a slave in America, *Uncle Tom's Cabin* would have taken hold upon the hearts of men, and moved to indignation just as it did with the case as it stood; and thus it is that, with the slavery issue long since dead, it has as many readers as ever. There are many books written with a mere local aim, which have risen on their merits above the causes that gave them birth, but of all these, *Uncle Tom's Cabin* is easily the most conspicuous case of a work written for purely local ends, outliving the reason of its creation and becoming an enduring fact in the world's literature.

At the close of the nineteenth century, Charles Dudley Warner praised *Uncle Tom's Cabin* as follows:

> The one indispensable requisite of a great work is its universality, its conception and construction so that it will appeal to universal human nature in all races and situations and climates. *Uncle Tom's Cabin* does that. Considering certain artistic deficiencies, which the French writers perceived, we might say that it was the timeliness of its theme that gave it currency in England and America. But that argument falls before the world-wide interest in it as a mere story, in so many languages, by races unaffected by our own relation to slavery.

By 1903 *A History of American Literature* referred to Harriet's writing deficiency (as compared to Jane Austen, George Eliot, and George Sand), but noted that *Uncle Tom* "is alive with emotion, and a book that is alive with emotion after the lapse of 50 years is a great book." Frank Luther Mott regarded *Uncle Tom's Cabin* as "a vital story, striking with extraordinary directness to the heart of fundamental feelings and relationships."

In the 1950s, Langston Hughes declared the book "a good story, exciting in incident, sharp in characterization, and threaded with humor." In his *Patriotic Gore*, Edmund Wilson wrote:

> Our of a background of undistinguished narrative, inelegantly and carelessly written, the characters leap into being with a vitality that is all the more striking for the ineptitude of the prose that presents them. These characters — like those of Dickens, at least in his early phase — express themselves a good deal better than the author expresses herself.

He saw "that a critical mind is at work, which has the complex situation in a very firm grip and which, no matter how vehement the characters become, is controlling and coordinating their interrelations."

Bruce Kirkham, an authority on *Uncle Tom's Cabin*, contended in 1965:

> There is little doubt but that *Uncle Tom's Cabin*, like Garrison's paper, is propoganda. Unlike *The Liberator*, it is also art. Both abolitionists sought reform and both employed emotion and logic to attain their ends, but Mrs. Stowe, unlike Garrison, saw the universal in the particular and by citing a detailed personal narrative related intimately to a nationally known incident she forced the public to participate, to become a slave.

The following year, an article in *Encounter* by Anthony Burgess noted that

> *Uncle Tom's Cabin* has been chiefly neglected — in our own age — because it is hard to accept that an instrument of historical change should also be a work of art.... Reading it, we find that all we have to forgive is the style.... Structurally, the book is very sound, and it even has a visual skeleton provided by the geography of slavery....

In his introduction to a 1967 edition of *Uncle Tom*, Robert Corrigan stated:

> Acclaimed by the average reader as a great book from the time of its first publication, it continues to be read by vast numbers throughout the world to this day, although it has been traditionally ignored and scorned by the professional literary critics. Recently, however, there has been evidence of the tide turning as increasing numbers of critics and scholars have begun to pay serious attention to this novel and reassess its place in the history of American letters.

By 1980, Jane Tompkins was explaining that in the 1960s she would not have dreamed of including *Uncle Tom's Cabin* as required reading for college English. "To begin with," she said, "its very popularity would have mitigated against it...." In 1969 a *Saturday Review of Literature* article by Kenneth Renroth expressed this view:

> It is absurd that in American universities there are countless courses in rhetorical, sentimental, and unreal novelists like James Fenimore Cooper or worse, and that this book, which played no small role in changing the history of the world, is passed over and misrepresented. Hawthorne, Cooper, Washington Irving ignore the reality of slavery. Yet slavery was the great fact of American life. Harriet Beecher Stowe alone of the major novelists faced the fact and worked out its consequences in the humanity

of those involved in it—master or slave or remote beneficiary. She knew that her New England was almost as dependent on the "peculiar institution" as any plantation owner.

By 1980, Milton Rugoff claimed that "at her best, Harriet Beecher Stowe was the first American realist of any consequence and the first to use fiction for a profound criticism of American society, especially its failure to live up to the promises of democracy."

The Library of America in 1982 saw fit to include Uncle Tom's Cabin along with the works of Melville, Hawthorne, and Whitman. Perhaps the tide is turning, as Professor Corrigan suggests.

The accuracy of Harriet's character portraits was attested to by a Union soldier who wrote about the southern Negroes he encountered: "I never saw a bunch of them together but I could pick out an Uncle Tom, a Quimbo, a Sambo, a Chloe, an Eliza or any other character in Uncle Tom's Cabin." Abolitionist tracts did not cite good masters, but Harriet portrayed good and bad Southerners, as she did good and bad blacks, never failing to point out that the system of slavery was evil. And some Southerners admitted that almost every shocking incident in the book could have happened, if it were not the norm. The vivid, dramatic fiction that Harriet produced appealed to readers' emotions far more than did the facts in abolitionist propaganda.

The modern reader dislikes the sentimentality of Uncle Tom. But the sentimental novel was popular in the nineteenth century, and Harriet deserves great credit for using it as a vehicle to portray the horrors of slavery. Charlotte Brontë admitted to shunning slavery as a subject for her novels; Frederika Brenner, the Swedish novelist and feminist, had wished to write about it while in the United States but failed to do so. Some lesser lights did produce fiction on this subject, but their efforts were not very effective. John Anthony Scott in his 1974 book, Hard Trials on My Way, noted Harriet's "lack of interest in exploring the psychological realities of oppression endured by black people—the experience of fear, sorrow, and rage that was the daily torment of the slave." Admittedly, this is a weakness in Uncle Tom's Cabin. Harriet's strength lay in letting blacks be seen through white eyes; so whites could identify with their plight. This is important because whites, not blacks, commanded political power.

The book's emphasis on religion, along with its sermon-like digressions, is foreign to the contemporary novel. As we have seen, however, religion played a prominent part in nineteenth-century life. The Beecher family was deeply immersed in this religion; so it is not surprising that Harriet's ideas on theology permeate *Uncle Tom*. It is even debatable whether she would have written the book without such religious fervor.

Some of the preaching is omitted in children's editions. For instance, Blackie's 1963 British edition omits the author's Preface and Concluding Remarks seen in regular editions. Perhaps the material is meaningless to young children, but it certainly is part and parcel of the book. Harriet must have considered children as members of her readership because she ended the last chapter in the *National Era* as follows:

> The "Author of Uncle Tom's Cabin" must now take leave of a wide circle of friends, whose faces she has never seen, but whose sympathies, coming to her from afar, have stimulated and cheered her work.
>
> The thought of the pleasant family circles that have been meeting in spirit weekly has been a constant refreshment to her, and she cannot leave them without a farewell.
>
> In particular, the dear little children who have followed her story have her warmest love. Dear children, you will one day be men and women; and she hopes that you will learn from this story always to remember and pity the poor and oppressed, and when you grow up, show your pity by doing all you can for them. Never, if you can help it, let a colored child be shut out of school, or treated with neglect or contempt, because of his color. Remember the sweet example of little Eva, and try to feel the same regard for all that she did; and then when you grow up, we hope that the foolish and unchristian prejudice against people, merely on account of their complexion, will be done away with.
>
> Farewell, dear children, till we meet again.

Social historians, as literary critics, are divided in opinion on *Uncle Tom*. The major criticisms came first from the South, then later from black Americans and also whites.

A long article in the *Southern Literary Messenger* of December, 1852, noted that Harriet's book, although professing to be fiction, had as its purpose proselytism. The article warns that "the tribunal to which our defence must be addressed is the public sentiment of the North and of Europe." (Harriet's main purpose had been to persuade slaveholders of the sin of holding their fellow men in bondage.)

By 1854 the South had turned out more than a dozen novels to refute *Uncle Tom's Cabin*. Of these, Mary H. Eastman's *Aunt*

Phyllis's Cabin or *Southern Life As It Is* was perhaps the best known. A comment in *Chambers's Edinburgh Journal* of February 5, 1853, expressed well the futility of this type of defense:

> A fiction, certainly, cannot give an authoritative view on any subject. It may, however, be legitimately useful in drawing attention to one. It strikes us, that the apologists of southern slavery take a poor and inefficient method of meeting Uncle Tom, by publishing fictions on the other side of the question. It is a mere chance that any of these has one-tenth part of the artistic excellence and effective eloquence of Mrs. Stowe's far-famed work.

Another approach was to criticize the authenticity of *Uncle Tom*. Valuable slaves like George Harris and Tom, the critics contended, would not be ill-treated; state law, in fact, usually protected slaves from extreme punishments. One critic objected that Harriet made southern ladies and gentlemen talk "rather vulgar Yankee-English" and her Louisiana Negroes talk "Kentuck." There were other trivial criticisms: Mr. Shelby would never have received a trader in his parlor, and Eva would not have been buried in the ground because persons of her status in New Orleans would have rated a burial vault. And so it went.

Writing 40 years after its publication, Francis Shoup, who fought for the Confederacy, said this about the book's reception in the South:

> Of course it was read by one here and there, but it is quite unusual, even now, to find a Southern-born man or woman, who has read it. When the question is asked, the reply as a rule is, "No, I never expect to read it." The conviction was that it was full of all manner of slanders and false statements about the South, and the feeling still prevails.

Southerners who did read *Uncle Tom's Cabin* must have recognized its potential effect on their "peculiar institution"; the following extracts from a diary show this. The writer is Charles Holbrook, a Northerner who was hired to tutor the children of a North Carolina planter named Gallaway:

> October 4, 1852. Finished "Uncle Tom's Cabin" this morning at recess! I believe it to be the most interesting book I ever read.... Ex, one of my pupils has told me this morning some things equal to any in that book....
> October 14, 1852. Mr. G. likes Uncle Toms Cabin but Mrs. G. is bitter against it.

October 15, 1852. Great talk in this house about Mrs. Stowe. Mr. G. is honest – he says he admires "Uncle Toms Cabin" for its true characters.

October 16, 1852. Mr. Gallaway says he will burn "Uncle Toms Cabin." He has changed his mind on it. Mrs. G. thinks Mrs. Stowe is worse than Legree!

Higginson in 1897 gave this insight into Harriet's representation of southern slavery:

> It is certain that many Southerners of high standing beginning with Senator Preston of South Carolina – in conversation with Professor Lieber – admitted that every fact *Uncle Tom's Cabin* contained might be duplicated from their own observation. All this might be true, however, and yet the general atmosphere of such a book might be unfair; there might be unfairness also in omissions.

Fair or not, southern author Thomas Nelson Page concluded that:

> By arousing the general sentiment of the world against slavery, *Uncle Tom's Cabin* contributed more than any one thing to its abolition in that generation ... and did more than any one thing that ever occurred to precipitate the war.

There was great interest in Harriet's sources for the book. She wrote in the Concluding Remarks:

> The separate incidents that compose the narrative are, to a very great extent, authentic, occurring, many of them, either under the writer's observation, or that of her personal friends. She or her friends have observed characters the counterpart of almost all that are here introduced; and many of the sayings are word for word as heard herself, or reported to her.

Harriet's explanations about prototypes for her characters were inconsistent. She declared in old age that Uncle Tom had no living prototype, while 40 years earlier she had said:

> I know a man now a slave in Kentucky – a worthy excellent soul, a devoted Christian who is the character from which I designed Uncle Tom – His wife lived with me for sometime as cook & I used to write her letters to him – It is true that he had the oversight of his masters business & the care of his horses and it is true that when he came over to see his wife who is a free woman living in Ohio & she tried to persuade him to run away that he

told her "Master *trusts* me & I cannot," yet his master has promised this man his liberty at Christmas for three years in succession & never kept his promise & I left him still a slave.

Twenty years earlier she told the same story, but also said that "other incidents were added by reading the life of Father Henson in Canada." *The Life of Josiah Henson, Formerly a Slave, Now an Inhabitant of Canada as Narrated by Himself* was published in Boston in 1849. Slave narratives like Henson's were popular with antislavery people, and Harriet was probably familiar with many. That same year saw two famous ones in print: *Narrative of the Life and Adventures of Henry Bibb, an American Slave, Written by Himself,* and *Narrative of William B. Brown, an American Slave.* In 1851 Harriet wrote to Frederick Douglass as follows:

> In the course of my story, the scene will fall upon a cotton plantation. I am very desirous hence to gain information from one who has been an actual laborer on one, and it occurred to me that in the circle of your acquaintance there might be one who would be able to communicate to me some such information as I desire....

She enclosed a list of questions to be answered and suggested that Henry Bibb might be helpful in supplying information. Obviously slave narratives would have been excellent source material for *Uncle Tom,* but just how Harriet used them is uncertain.

As mentioned earlier, Charles Beecher had described to his sister an individual from which she derived Legree—a man who boasted that his fist was "calloused with knocking down niggers." Harriet stated in *The Key*:

> Legree is introduced not for the sake of vilifying masters as a class, but for the sake of bringing to the minds of honorable Southern men, who are masters, a very important feature in the system of slavery, upon which, perhaps, they have never reflected. It is this: that *no Southern law requires any test of CHARACTER from the man to whom the absolute power of master is granted.*

St. Clare was created "with enthusiasm and with hope" that a Southerner will rise up and free his land from "the burden and disgrace of slavery." We note that St. Clare, a Southerner, is, like the infidel Saladin in *The Talisman,* treated sympathetically. (Harriet had read this novel of Scott's in 1850.)

Emmeline and Cassy were inspired by two beautiful mulatto girls named Mary and Emily Edmondson. Henry Ward Beecher was instrumental in raising money to purchase their freedom. Miss Ophelia, according to her creator, is "the representative of a numerous class of the very best of northern people...."

Eliza, as noted in *Uncle Tom's Cabin*, was drawn from life. There is some evidence that in the 1830s Harriet had heard of the successful flight of a slave woman with her child across the frozen Ohio River from Kentucky to Ripley, Ohio. She also said she had read about such an event in an antislavery magazine. Harriet wrote in 1885:

> Some events in the life of Lewis Clarke are somewhat like some in the story of George Harris. I read his history while writing the story merely to see that I was keeping within the limits of probability.

According to *The Key*, she learned in Kentucky "that a young colored man invented a machine for cleaning hemp, like that alluded to in *Uncle Tom's Cabin*."

Eva, according to her originator, was the "impersonation in childish form of the love of Christ." The model for Van Tromp was John Van Zant, a former Kentucky slave owner. According to Harriet, he freed his slaves and moved to Ohio, where he often harbored fugitives. In 1846 slaveholders were successful in suing him for this.

Some of Harriet's descendants identified Topsy as the child of a family that became free when the owners moved from Louisiana to Ohio and whom Harriet taught in a Sunday School.

From these examples, it is clear that Harriet proceeded as any fiction writer — weaving experience, fact, and fantasy to produce a vibrant story with an authentic background. Many critics believe she was influenced by Scott and Dickens in particular, as well as by the women of her generation who authored sentimental novels. She was not producing a treatise on slavery or biographical sketches of its victims and was therefore at liberty to use her imagination. But *Uncle Tom's Cabin* is primarily a message. If the reader failed to see it in the story line, he could scarcely miss it in the discourses present throughout the book.

From the beginning, there were critics who objected to Harriet's treatment of the Negro, and this criticism reached its height in the twentieth century. It is well expressed by Philip Van Doren Stern in his introduction to a 1964 edition of *Uncle Tom's Cabin*:

> During the last few decades, more and more people, white as well as black, became increasingly aware of the fact that stereotypes of Negro behavior were hurting his efforts to escape from the inferior role that had been thrust upon him. The happy-go-lucky, shallow-pated, subservient creature who spoke in a thick dialect was no longer an acceptable representation of the black man. White people had had to admit that the Negroes they saw around them had almost nothing in common with those in *Uncle Tom's Cabin* or with others portrayed in the past.
>
> As a result, Negroes themselves began to resent the Uncle Tom image. That this image was derived more from shoddy, unauthorized Tom shows than from the book itself is beside the point. Uncle Tom became synonymous with servility, and Negroes began to hate the book which had helped set them free.

In 1945 an Uncle Tom play was temporarily banned in Bridgeport, Connecticut, because "it refreshed memories that tend to portray only weaknesses of a racial minority, and hold up to ridicule peoples who in the early days of our country were unfortunately subjected to exposures that today would be considered atrocious." The next year, a poll conducted by *Negro Digest* showed that a majority of blacks considered the play anti-Negro since it presented the black in a submissive, docile, cringing role, portraying him as less than a man.

Brion Gysin, author of an anti-*Uncle Tom* book entitled *To Master — A Long Goodbye* (1946) stated that "Uncle Tom is the ghost of a certain relationship between the races in America, and as he marches toward the second half of the twentieth century, he is a ghost which must be laid."

Almost a hundred years after the publication of *Uncle Tom's Cabin*, author James Baldwin was scathing in his criticism of the book's portrayal of the Negro — especially with regard to Uncle Tom's humility. Baldwin also termed *Uncle Tom's Cabin* a catalogue of violence that left unanswered and unnoticed the only important question: What motivated such deeds?

Joseph Furnas, who wrote *Goodbye to Uncle Tom* in 1956, accused Harriet of racist teachings and pointed out the damage caused by her engraved stereotypes of meek and obsequious blacks: "...we all still see Negroes and their plight all too consistently through Mrs. Stowe's flawed and long-obsolete spectacles."

Writing in the *New Republic* in 1963, Hugh Alfred Taylor objected to *Uncle Tom's Cabin* because it may "reinforce unfavorable stereotypes of Negroes and encourage condescending pity instead of desperately needed mutual respect and fellowship." He also declared that

> Unwittingly, Mrs. Stowe did her full share of encouraging Northern indifference to the 1877 takeover by the Southern White Redeemers that enthroned Jim Crow laws and abased Negroes to the lowest level of their four centuries as Americans.

Taylor brought up other points that have disturbed readers: Harriet suggested colonization for freed blacks (Garrison, for instance, objected vigorously to this), and she represented George, Eliza, Cassy, and Emmeline, all of whom are smart enough to escape, as almost white. (Jean Yellin in *The Intricate Knot: Black Figures in American Literature, 1776–1863* [1972] noted that Harriet's black people are inevitably subservient, while mulattoes combine the sensitivity of their black mothers with the strength of their white fathers.)

Alex Haley, of *Roots* fame, writing in 1964, made this comment:

> Mrs. Stowe's novel, for all its faults, is redeemed by the fact that it helped to end the institution of slavery. It is a deep irony that a century later, the very name of Mrs. Stowe's hero is the worst insult the slaves' descendants can hurl at one another out of their frustrations in seeking what all other Americans take for granted.

Again with regard to race relations, a critical essay by Thomas Riggio in 1976 reminded us that *Uncle Tom's Cabin* was directly responsible for Thomas Dixon's racist novel *The Leopard's Spots* (1902), which sold more than a million copies and was based on the assumption of white superiority.

In addition to criticisms of the book itself, Harriet's earnings from *Uncle Tom's Cabin* brought her personal censure. Dumond, in his *Antislavery*, stated, "Whether she or the antislavery cause profited most from her writing is a moot question." (In a capitalistic society, denigration of the profit motive is curious indeed.) In *Trumpets of Jubilee* (1927), Constance Rourke declared: "At a stroke she reaped the reward of the long and arduous labors accomplished through more than 20 years by that small group of iconoclasts whose leader was Garrison." Others have added that these iconoclasts suffered scorn, ridicule, and worse, while Harriet reaped profit and fame.

On balance, social historians regard *Uncle Tom's Cabin* positively. In 1852 the following statement appeared in the *New York Post*: "There are but two courses to which we can look for the extinction of slavery, first the interest of the planters, and secondly, the power of public opinion." Harriet failed to move the planters, but she was overwhelmingly successful in changing public opinion. This success continues to be recognized: At its centenary, *Uncle Tom's Cabin* was termed by the Modern Library "certainly the most influential book ever written in America." In 1954 historian Eric Goldman listed *Uncle Tom* among 13 books which have changed America. He drew attention to the broad impact of the book, "with its harnessing of Christianity and democracy into a appeal for all the disadvantaged." In 1970 librarian Robert Downs included it and Myrdal's *An American Dilemma* among 25 books that changed the nation.

The following are a few examples of how *Uncle Tom* moved specific persons to social action. This was written by Alex Ross, a Canadain physician-ornithologist:

> While I was engaged in my inquiries among the colored people of Canada, Mrs. Stowe's work, *Uncle Tom's Cabin*, was published and excited the sympathies of every humane person who read it, in behalf of the oppressed. To me it was a command; and a settled conviction took possession of my mind, that it was my duty to help the oppressed to freedom....

Ross carried out his resolution, helping slaves escape to Canada from Memphis, New Orleans, Augusta, and other places in the South. *Uncle Tom's Cabin* was the spur for Alexander II of Russia to free 20 million serfs, and the impetus for a lady of high rank in the Court of Siam to liberate her 130 slaves.

In 1945, when the question of banning Uncle Tom plays came up, John Mason Brown wrote in the *Saturday Review*: "Certainly the Negro is not what he was when Mrs. Stowe wrote. Mrs. Stowe is one of those who must be thanked because he is not."

In a 1962 article in the *New Statesman*, Dan Jacobson made these interesting comments:

> It does not seem to me to be impunging the dignity of the passive resistors in the deep South, or that of Mr. James Meredith, to say that their actions have something in common with Uncle Tom's.

Perhaps the worst thing about *Uncle Tom's Cabin* is that Mrs. Stowe never fully imagined that the day would come when Negroes would read her novel and comment on it; she never appeared to have asked herself what her university-educated George Harris, for example, would have made of her "kindly" references to his race, or to Uncle Tom's martyrdom. In view of the cause she was pleading, this failure of imagination is obviously a crucial one; and one for which she is less and less likely to be forgiven in the future. However, we can trust her sufficiently to say that she would not have minded at all.

Today's mature reader knows from experience that the black is as capable as the white if given opportunity. That reader is likely to be familiar with the artistry of Leontyne Price, the eloquence of Barbara Jordan, and the vision of Martin Luther King, Jr. He does not consider Tom or Topsy representative of today's Negro any more than he considers Ophelia a product of modern New England or Eva a typical child of today's South. So the argument about fixed stereotypes is weakened and will continue to be weakened.

As to the criticism that the more clever characters are light enough not to be recognized as slaves, fiction writers are seldom required to defend the complexions of their creations. But it should be noted that miscegenation was a fact of life in the South, and Harriet used pale Negroes such as Eliza and Cassy to emphasize that white masters did violate black women. (Judith Berson in her *Neither White nor Black: The Mulatto Character in American Fiction* (1978) stated that "Cassy is a powerful weapon in Mrs. Stowe's war against slavery and injustice.") Another reason that Harriet used light Negroes may have been that their color made it easier for them to escape, and, after all, a fiction writer is entitled to create such people. Here is John Scott's comment on *Uncle Tom's Cabin* (1974):

No, the thrust of the *Cabin* did not lie in its radical vision of an American interracial future; it lay elsewhere.... It was a call to Americans ... to recognize simply that the holding of men and women in bondage, regardless of race, creed, or color was *wrong* and must stop.... She announced, and she demanded, a revolution in American public opinion.... American opinion was ripe for the revolution. It was due largely to Mrs. Stowe that it occurred exactly when it did. The sectional collision loomed. She translated it into human and moral terms that millions of ordinary people could feel, measure, and understand.

Simon Legree, Eliza crossing the ice, Uncle Tom, Topsy, and Eva are now part of our national culture. Even as late as 1928, a movie version of *Uncle Tom's Cabin* was made, while *The King and I*, the still-popular musical by Rogers and Hammerstein, includes a ballet entitled *The Small House of Uncle Thomas*. People continue to read this book that had its day more than a century ago. Perhaps this is not unusual, because, according to Corrigan, "It has a combination of Christian message, political reform, engaging characters, exciting action, and the continuing confrontation between good and evil. If for no other reason than its contribution to the antislavery movement in America, it would deserve a well-earned place in our history books."

And Stern contends that to read *Uncle Tom's Cabin* is a necessary part of one's education, important in tracing the emergence of the present from the past.

We agree, and fervently hope that in the event of a future national crisis, another Harriet Beecher Stowe will come forth to produce a book or a documentary or a television play with the force of *Uncle Tom's Cabin*.

Selected Bibliography

Books

Abbott, Shirley. *The National Museum of American History*. New York: Abrams, 1981.

Adams, F.C. *Uncle Tom at Home: A Review of the Reviewers and Repudiators of Uncle Tom's Cabin by Mrs. Stowe*. Freeport, NY: Books for Libraries Press, reprinted 1970. First published 1853.

Alderman, Clifford Lindsey. *Colonists for Sale: The Story of Indentured Servants in America*. New York: Macmillan, 1975.

_____. *Rum, Slaves and Molasses: The Story of New England's Triangular Trade*. Folkstone, England: Bailey & Swinfen, 1974.

*Ammons, Elizabeth. *Critical Essays on Harriet Beecher Stowe*. Boston: G.K. Hall, 1980.

*Ashton, Jean W. *Harriet Beecher Stowe: A Reference Guide*. Boston: G.K. Hall, 1977.

Barker-Benfield, G.J. *The Horrors of the Half-Known Life: Male Attitudes toward Women and Sexuality in Nineteenth-Century America*. New York: Harper & Row, 1976.

Bartlett, Irving H. *The American Mind in Mid-Nineteenth Century*. Northbrook, IL: AHM, 1967.

Berky, Andrew S. and Shenton, James P. (eds.). *The Historians' History of the United States* Vol. 1. New York: Capricorn, 1966.

Berzon, Judith R. *Neither White nor Black: The Mulatto Character in American Fiction*. New York: New York University, 1978.

Birney, Catherine H. *The Grimké Sisters*. Boston: Lee & Shepard, 1885.

Blassingame, John W. *The Slave Community: Plantation Life in the Antebellum South*. New York: Oxford, 1979.

Bode, Carl (ed.). *American Life in the 1840s*. New York: New York University, 1967.

Bontemps, Arna (introduction). *Five Black Lives: The Autobiographies of Venture Smith, James Mars, William Grimes, The Rev. G.W. Offley, James L. Smith*. Middleton, CT: Wesleyan University, 1971.

_____. (ed.). *Great Slave Narratives*. Boston: Beacon, 1969.

*Boorstin, Daniel J. *The Americans: The National Experience*. New York: Random House, 1965.

*Brady, Terence and Jones, Evan. *The Fight Against Slavery*. New York: Norton, 1975.

Buckmaster, Henrietta. *Let My People Go*. New York: Harper, 1941.

*These publications proved very helpful with regard to the scope of this book.

Burwell, Letitia M. *A Girl's Life in Virginia before the War*. New York: Stokes, 1895.

Catt, Nancy F. (ed.). *Root of Bitterness*. New York: Dutton, 1972.

Chesnut, Mary Boykin. *A Diary from Dixie*. New York: Appleton, 1905.

Child, Lydia M. *The American Frugal Housewife*. Boston: American Stationers', 1829.

Craven, Avery. *The Coming of the Civil War*. 2nd ed., rev. Chicago: University of Chicago, 1957.

Davis, David Brion. *The Problem of Slavery in the Age of Revolution, 1770–1823*. Ithaca, NY: Cornell University, 1975.

————. *The Problem of Slavery in Western Culture*. Ithaca, NY: Cornell University, 1966.

Delano, Alonzo. *Life in the Plains and among the Diggings*. New York: Readex Microprint, 1966. First published 1854.

Donald, David. *Charles Sumner and the Coming of the Civil War*. New York: Knopf, 1960.

————. *Lincoln Reconsidered*. New York: Knopf, 1956.

Downs, Robert B. *Books That Changed America*. New York: Macmillan, 1970.

Drepperd, Carl W. *Pioneer America: Its First Three Centuries*. Garden City, NY: Doubleday, 1949.

Dublin, Thomas (ed.) *Farm to Factory: Women's Letters, 1830–1860*. New York: Columbia University, 1981.

Du Bois, William E.B. *The Souls of Black Folk*. From *Three Negro Classics*. New York: Avon, 1965. First published 1903.

*Dumond, Dwight Lowell. *Antislavery: The Crusade for Freedom in America*. Ann Arbor, MI: University of Michigan, 1961.

Elkins, Stanley M. *Slavery: A Problem in American Institutional and Intellectual Life*. 3rd ed., rev. Chicago: University of Chicago, 1976.

Faust, Drew Gilpin. *A Sacred Circle: The Dilemma of the Intellectual in the Old South, 1840–1860*. Baltimore: Johns Hopkins University, 1977.

Fiedler, Leslie A. *The Inadvertent Epic: From Uncle Tom's Cabin to Roots*. New York: Simon & Schuster, 1979.

Fields, Annie. *Life and Letters of Harriet Beecher Stowe*. Boston: Houghton Mifflin, 1897.

*Filler, Louis. *The Crusade Against Slavery*. New York: Harper & Row, 1960.

Fladeland, Betty. *Men and Brothers: Anglo-American Antislavery Cooperation*. Urbana, IL: University of Illinois, 1972.

Foster, Charles B. *The Rungless Ladder: Harriet Beecher Stowe and New England Puritanism*. Durham, NC: Duke University, 1954.

Franklin, John Hope. *From Slavery to Freedom: A History of Negro Americans*. 5th ed. New York: Knopf, 1980.

————. *A Southern Odyssey: Travelers in the Antebellum North*. Baton Rouge, LA: Louisiana State University, 1976.

Frederickson, George M. *Great Lives Observed: William Lloyd Garrison*. Englewood Cliffs, NJ: Prentice-Hall, 1968.

Frothingham, Paul Revere. *Edward Everett: Orator and Statesman*. Port Washington, NY: Kennikat, 1971. First published 1925.

Furnas, Joseph C. *Goodbye to Uncle Tom*. New York: Sloan, 1956.

Gara, Larry. *The Liberty Line*. Lexington: University of Kentucky, 1961.

Gerson, Noel B. *Harriet Beecher Stowe: A Biography*. New York: Praeger, 1976.

Gilbertson, Catherine. *Harriet Beecher Stowe*. New York: Appleton-Century, 1937.

*Gruver, Rebecca Brooks. *An American History*. Vol. 1. to 1877. Vol. 2 from 1865 to the present. Reading, MA: Addison-Wesley, 1972.

Gysin, Brion. *To Master—A Long Goodnight*. New York: Creative Age, 1946.

Hall, Arethusa. *Life and Character of the Rev. Sylvester Judd*. Port Washington, NY: Kennikat, 1971. First published 1854.

Haller, John S. and Haller, Robin M. *The Physician and Sexuality in Victorian America*. Urbana, IL: University of Illinois, 1974.

*Hart, Albert Bushnell. *Slavery and Abolition, 1831–41*. New York: Negro Universities Press, 1968. First published 1906.

Hecker, Eugene A. *A Short History of Women's Rights*. 2nd ed. revised, with additions. Westport, CT: Greenwood, 1971.

Hersh, Blanche Glassman. *The Slavery of Sex: Feminist-Abolitionists in America*. Urbana: University of Illinois, 1978.

Hewitt, James (ed.) *Eye-Witnesses to Wagon Trains West*. New York: Scribner, 1973.

*Hildreth, Margaret Holbrook. *Harriet Beecher Stowe: A Bibliography*. Hamden, CT: Shoe String, 1976.

Horan, James D. *Mathew Brady: Historian with a Camera*. New York: Bonanza, 1955.

Hymowitz, Carol and Weissman, Michaele. *A History of Women in America*. New York: Bantam, 1978.

Johnson, Johanna. *Runaway to Heaven: The Story of Harriet Beecher Stowe and Her Era*. New York: Doubleday, 1963.

*Jorgenson, Chester E. (ed.). *Uncle Tom's Cabin As Book and Legend: A Guide to an Exhibition*. Detroit: Friends of Detroit Public Library, 1952.

*Kirkham, E. Bruce. *The Building of Uncle Tom's Cabin*. Knoxville: University of Tennessee, 1977.

*Lacour-Gayet, Robert. *Everyday Life in the United States before the Civil War, 1830–60*. New York: Fred. Ungar, 1969.

Lerner, Gerda. *The Female Experience: An American Documentary*. Indianapolis: Bobbs-Merrill, 1977.

_____. *The Grimké Sisters from South Carolina*. Boston: Houghton Mifflin, 1967.

Lillibridge, G.D. *Images of American Society: A History of the United States*. Vol. 1. Boston: Houghton Mifflin, 1976.

Litwack, Leon F. *Been in the Storm So Long: The Aftermath of Slavery*. New York: Knopf, 1979.

Lumpkin, Katherine Du Pre. *The Emancipation of Angelina Grimké*. Chapel Hill: University of North Carolina, 1974.

_____. *The Making of a Southerner* (1946). Athens: University of Georgia, 1981.

Lynes, Russell. *The Domesticated Americans*. New York: Harper & Row, 1957.

Mabee, Carleton. *Black Freedom: The Nonviolent Abolitionists from 1830 through the Civil War*. New York: Macmillan, 1970.

*Mair, Margaret G. and Royce, Diana. *The Papers of Harriet Beecher Stowe*. Earl A. French (ed.). Hartford, CT: Stowe-Day Foundation, 1977.

Marshall, Dorothy. *Fanny Kemble*. New York: St. Martin, 1977.

Martin, Bernard. *John Newton: A Biography*. London: Wm. Heinemann, 1950.

Miller, Eilinor and Genovese, D. (eds.). *Plantation, Town, and County: Essays on the Local History of American Slave Society*. Urbana: Univ. of Illinois, 1974.

Moers, Ellen. *Harriet Beecher Stowe and American Literature*. Hartford, CT: Stowe-Day Foundation, 1978.

Nash, Gary B. (ed.). *The Private Side of American History*. Vol. I to 1877. New York: Harcourt Brace Jovanovich, 1975.

Nye, Russel B. *William Lloyd Garrison and the Humanitarian Reformers*. Boston: Little, Brown, 1855.

Oates, Stephen B. *To Purge This Land with Blood: A Biography of John Brown*. New York: Harper & Row, 1970.

_____. *With Malice Toward None: The Life of Abraham Lincoln*. New York: Harper & Row, 1977.

Olmsted, Frederick Law. *The Papers of Frederick Law Olmsted*. Vol. II—*Slavery and the South 1852–1857*. Charles E. Beveridge and Charles C. McLaughlin (eds.). Baltimore: Johns Hopkins University, 1981.

Ossoli, S. Margaret. *Woman in the Nineteenth Century and Kindred Papers...* Arthur B. Fuller (ed.). Boston: c. 1855.

*Pease, William H. and Pease, Jane H. (eds.). *The Antislavery Argument*. Indianapolis: Bobbs-Merrill, 1965.

Perry, Lewis and Fellman, Michael. *Antislavery Reconsidered: New Perspectives on the Abolitionists*. Baton Rouge: Louisiana State University, 1979.

Preston, Dickson J. *Young Frederick Douglass: The Maryland Years*. Baltimore: Johns Hopkins University, 1980.

Quint, Howard; Albertson, Dean; and Cantor, Milton (eds.). *Main Problems in American History*. Vol. 1, rev. ed. Homewood, IL: Dorsey, 1968.

Randel, William Peirce. *The Evolution of American Taste: The History of American Style from 1607 to the Present*. New York: Crown, 1978.

Redding, Saunders. *They Came in Chains*. Rev. ed. Philadelphia: Lippincott, 1973. First published 1950.

Reed, James. *From Private Vice to Public Virtue: The Birth Control Movement and American Society Since 1830*. New York: Basic Books, 1978.

Roller, D.C. and Twyman, R.W. (eds.). *Encyclopedia of Southern History*. Baton Rouge: Louisiana State University, 1979.

Rosen, George. *A History of Public Health*. New York: MD, 1958.

Ross, Alexander Milton. *Recollections and Experiences of an Abolitionist (1855–65)*. Northbrook, IL: Metro, 1972.

*Rothman, David J. and Rothman, Sheila M. (eds.). *Sources of the American Social Tradition*. New York: Basic Books, 1975.

*Rugoff, Milton. *The Beechers*. New York: Harper & Row, 1981.

Saum, Lewis O. *The Popular Mind of Pre-Civil War America*. Westport, CT: Greenwood, 1980.

Scott, John Anthony. *Hard Trials on My Way: Slavery and the Struggle Against It 1800–1860*. New York: Knopf, 1974.

Sherwin, Oscar. *Prophet of Liberty: The Life and Times of Wendell Phillips*. New York: Bookman Assoc., 1958.

Sinclair, William A. *The Aftermath of Slavery* (1905). New York: Arno, 1969.

Sklar, Kathryn Kish. *Catherine Beecher*. New Haven: Yale University, 1973.

Smith, Elbert B. *The Death of Slavery: The United States, 1837–65*. Daniel Boorstin (ed.). Chicago: University of Chicago, 1967.

Stampp, Kenneth M. *The Imperiled Union*. New York: Oxford, 1980.

Stowe, Charles E. *Life of Harriet Beecher Stowe*. Boston: Houghton Mifflin, 1889.

*Stowe, Harriet Beecher. *The Key to Uncle Tom's Cabin*. New York: Arno, 1969. First published 1854.

*_____. *Uncle Tom's Cabin* (1851–52). New York: Pocket Books, 1963.

Stowe, Lyman Beecher. *Saints, Sinners and Beechers*. Indianapolis: Bobbs-Merrill, 1934.

Stratton, Joanna L. *Pioneer Women: Voices from the Kansas Frontier*. New York: Simon & Schuster, 1981.

Tocqueville, Alexis de. *Democracy in America*. George Lawrence (tr.). J.P. Mayer and Max Lerner (eds.). New York: Harper & Row, 1966. First published 1835.

Thomas, Benjamin P. *Theodore Weld: Crusader for Freedom*. New Brunswick, NJ: Rutgers University, 1950.

Unrah, John P., Jr. *The Plains Across: The Overland Emigrants and the Trans-Mississippi West 1840–60*. Urbana: University of Illinois, 1979.

Wagenknecht, Edward. *Harriet Beecher Stowe: The Known and the Unknown*. New York: Oxford, 1965.

*Walker, Robert H. *The Reform Spirit in America: A Documentation of the Pattern of Reform in the American Republic.* New York: Putnam, 1976.

Walters, Ronald G. *The Antislavery Appeal: American Abolitionism after 1830.* Baltimore: Johns Hopkins University, 1976.

Washington, Booker T. *Up from Slavery.* In *Three Negro Classics.* New York: Avon, 1970. First published 1901.

Weinstein, Allen; Gatell, Frank O.; and Sarasohn, David. *American Negro Slavery: A Modern Reader.* 3rd ed. New York: Oxford, 1979.

*Weld, Theodore Dwight. *American Slavery As It Is: Testimony of a Thousand Witnesses.* New York: Arno, 1969. First published anonymously 1839.

Williams, Eric. *Capitalism and Slavery.* New York: Capricorn, 1966. First published 1944.

Wilson, Edmund. *Patriotic Gore: Studies of the Literature of the American Civil War.* New York: Oxford, 1962.

*Wilson, Forrest. *Crusader in Crinoline: The Life of Harriet Beecher Stowe.* Philadelphia: Lippincott, 1941.

Wish, Harvey (ed.). *Ante-Bellum: Writings of George Fitzhugh and Hinton Rowan Helper on Slavery.* New York: Putnam, 1960.

Wright, Louis B. *Life on the American Frontier.* New York: Capricorn, 1971. First published 1968.

Yellin, Jean Fagan. *The Intricate Knot: Black Figures in American Literature 1776–1863.* New York: New York University, 1972.

Articles, Introductions, and Afterwords

Brown, John Mason. "Topsy-Turvy." *Sat. Rev. Lit.*, Oct. 6, 1945, pp. 24–25.

Corrigan, Robert. (Introduction) *Uncle Tom's Cabin.* New York: Airmont, 1967.

Clough, Wilson O. "A Journal of Village Life in Vermont in 1848." *N.E. Quart.*, Jan. 1928, pp. 32–34.

Crandall, John C. "Patriotism and Humanitarianism Reforms in Children's Literature 1825–1860." *Am. Quart.*, 1969, pp. 313–22.

Dempsey, David. "'Uncle Tom,' Centenarian." *New York Times Mag.*, June 3, 1951, pp. 55–56.

Douglas, Ann. "The Art of Controversy." (Introduction) *Uncle Tom's Cabin.* New York: Penguin, 1981.

Goldman, Eric P. "Books That Changed America." *Sat. Rev. Lit.*, July 4, 1953, p. 7.

Haley, Alex. "In 'Uncle Tom' Are Our Guilt and Hope." *New York Times Mag.*, March 1, 1964, p. 23.

Hall, D.D. "A Yankee Tutor in the Old South." *N.E. Quart.*, March, 1960, pp. 82–90.

Higginson, Thomas W. Obituary of Harriet Beecher Stowe. *Nation*, July 9, 1896, pp. 24–26.

Hoffert, Sylvia. "This 'One Great Evil'." *Am. Hist. Ill.*, May, 1977, pp. 37–41.

Iglesias, Antonio. "The Classic Blend in Literature." *Sat. Rev. Lit.*, Jan. 14, 1950, pp. 6–8.

Jacobson, Dan. "Down the River." *New Statesman*, Oct. 12, 1962, pp. 490–91.

Jewitt, John P. Posthumous publications about *Uncle Tom's Cabin. East Orange (NJ) Record*, Nov. 20, Nov. 27, Dec. 4, Dec. 11, Dec. 18, 1947.

"Just Growed Again." *Newsweek*, June 14, 1948, p. 98.

Kaufman, Martin. "'Step Right Up, Ladies and Gentlemen...' Patent Medicines in 19th-Century America." *Am. Hist. Ill.*, Aug., 1981, pp. 38–45.

Lee, Wallace. "Is 'Uncle Tom's Cabin' Anti-Negro?" *Negro Digest*, Jan. 1946, pp. 68–72.

Lippman, Theo, Jr. "Stowe's Work Belongs to U.S. History." *Baltimore Sun*, June 14, 1982.

Lynn, Kenneth S. "Mrs. Stowe and the American Imagination." *New Republic*, June 29, 1963, pp. 20–21.

McGinty, Brian. "A Heap o' Trouble." *Am. Hist. Ill.*, May, 1981, pp. 34–39.

Melcher, F.G. "America's No. 1 Best Seller Reaches a Centenary." *Pubs. Weekly*, March 14, 1952, p. 1290.

Monroe, Kirk. Introduction. *The Lives and Deeds of Our Self-Made Men*. Boston: Estes & Laureat, 1889.

Moody, Richard. "Uncle Tom,' the Theater and Mrs. Stowe." *Am. Heritage*, Oct. 1955, pp. 29–32.

Munson, J.E.B. "Uncle Tom' in England." *Civil War Times*, Jan. 1983, pp. 40–43.

Patee, Fred L. (ed.). "The Feminine Fifties." (Pages 130–145 on *Uncle Tom's Cabin*.) New York: Appleton-Century, 1940.

Randall, David and Winterich, John. "One Hundred Good Novels." *Pubs. Weekly*, May 18, 1940, pp. 1931–33.

Rexroth, Kenneth. "Uncle Tom's Cabin." *Sat. Rev. Lit.*, Jan. 11, 1969, p. 71.

Smith, Harrison. "Feminism and the Household Novel." *Sat. Rev. Lit.*, March 30, 1957, p. 22.

Showalter, Elaine. "Responsibilities and Realities: A Curriculum for the Eighties." *ADE Bull.*, Winter, 1981, pp. 17–21.

Spinney, Frank O. "A New Hampshire Schoolmaster Views Kentucky: Three Letters, 1847–48." *N.E. Quart.*, March, 1944.

Stern, Philip Van Dorn. Introduction. *The Annotated "Uncle Tom's Cabin."* New York: Bramhall, 1964.

Stowe, Harriet Beecher. "The Story of 'Uncle Tom's Cabin'." *Old South Leaflets*, 4, (82). Boston, 1897. First published 1878.

Taylor, Alfred Hugh. "Uncle Tom's Cabin." *New Republic*, July 13, 1963, p. 21.

Tompkins, Jane P. "Sentimental Power: 'Uncle Tom's Cabin' and the Politics of Literary History." *Glyph*, Vol. 8, 1980, pp. 70–102.

*"Uncle Tom's Cabin." (? George Frederick Holmes.) *Southern Lit. Messenger*, Oct. 1952, pp. 630–38. *Ibid.*, 721–31. Dec. 1852.

"The 'Uncle Tom' Excitement." *Chambers's Edinburgh Jour.*, Feb. 5, 1853, p. 85.

"'Uncle Tom's' Message." *London Times Literary Supplement*, Oct. 4, 1963, pp. 777–78.

Ward, John William. Afterword. *Uncle Tom's Cabin*. New York: NAL, 1966.

Wiley, Bell I. "The Spurned Teachers from Yankeedom." *Am. Hist. Ill.*, Feb. 1980, pp. 14–19.

Wilson, Edmund. "No! No! My Soul A'nt Yours, Mas'r!'" *New Yorker*, Nov. 27, 1948, pp. 134–38.

"The Woman Suffrage Plank." (Letter from Cincinnati.) *New York Herald*, June 16, 1876.

Index